From Inside Out

**An account of all the prisoners
hanged at H.M.P. Belfast**

Johnston J. Fitzgerald

ISBN 0 - 9519261 - 7 - 9

Set and formatted on 10 point Palatino (Normal)
on an Apple Macintosh II

From The Inside Out

An account of all the prisoners hanged at H.M.P. Belfast

CONTENTS

I have included other murders of general interest in Northern Ireland :-

2

Acknowledgements

I would like to thank Mr. B. Moore, Deputy Governor of Hydebank Young Offenders Centre for his help and encouragement when I first began my research for this book.

Mr. James Poots MA (Hons.), who edited my manuscript. The staff of the various libraries that I used and whose patience and understanding I am grateful, also spring to mind.

My thanks also go out to all those prison officers with whom I have had the pleasure of working. Many have either gone into retirement or died since I began my project. Without their endless information I would never have got as far as I did.

Last but not least I wish to thank my wife Jean, who had to put up with my frequent long absences. Her help in going through yesteryear's newspapers were much appreciated.

I am sure I have forgotten the names of many others who helped me along the way. A big thank you goes out to all of them. You know who you are.

Preface

In my nineteen years as a prison officer, from March 1974 to the present day, I have had the opportunity to study murderers at close quarters. Most of these murderers, however, would claim that their crimes are of a 'political' nature. The question I often find myself asking is : how many of these so-called 'political murderers' would have murdered if it had not been for the 'troubles?'

The seventeen murderers whose stories are told here were all hanged in H.M.P. Belfast or 'Antrim Prison,' as it was called in its early days. I would describe them all as 'amateurs' ; none of them, prior to their single acts of madness, had lived anything other than perfectly ordinary lives. Williams, perhaps, could be excluded from this category.

These hangings occurred between 1854 and 1961, a period of 107 years - an average of one execution every six years.

Since Northern Ireland's present 'Troubles' began twenty-five years ago, there have been over three thousand murders. Not all of the murderers have been brought to justice, and none have been executed.

Prior to the 'Sixties', murders were major talking-points, headline news for weeks and even longer. Every murder case was reported from beginning to end : arrest, trail(s), sentence, appeal, execution, inquest.

Today, murders are nine-day wonders ; sporadic occurrences in a seemingly never-ending cycle of violence and counter-violence. We have grown used to what has been described as an 'acceptable level of violence.'

Johnston J. Fitzgerald
Hydebank Young Offender's Centre,
August 1993

The reasons why I decided to compile a book on H.M.P. Belfast

Before I joined the Northern Ireland Prison Service I used to drive past H.M.P. Belfast and wonder 'what goes on inside there? and what does a warder really do?' I never thought for a moment that I would be one someday.

The first day of my new career I shall never forget. When they closed the large doors behind me I remember thinking to myself 'I will never stick this job' - mainly because of the claustrophobic effect. But here I am 20 years later, still plodding on.

At that early stage, writing a book about H.M.P. Belfast was far from my mind.

I have worked in H.M.P. Belfast, H.M.P. Maze, Millisle Borstal, H.M.P. Magilligan and of course the Young Offender's Centre, Belfast.

It was during the period of time I spent in H.M.P. Belfast, which was from 1980 until 1983 that I came across some old records and discovered after reading them that they were full of interesting facts. I got permission to go through all the old records in this store, and it was then that I decided to write a book or books about the penal system. Although this book is mainly on H.M.P. Belfast and the individuals who were executed there.

All of my script had to go through the Northern Ireland Office to be checked, just in case it contained something detrimental to the Prison Service. I have found them most helpful.

I never dreamt that over a period of two years, my research would have taken me to Florida's Law University, the Linenhall Library, Belfast, the National Library Dublin (which put up with me for two days at a time) and last but not least Belfast Central Library.

Proper research costs not only a lot of time and money but also a lot of patience and an understanding wife.

I have covered all the hangings in H.M.P. Crumlin Road Belfast and some other hangings of a historical nature.

I discovered that there was a void of information about the hangings from 1901 back. The reason for this was as the law which made it compulsory to register all deaths, births and marriages did not come into being until 1900/1901 which meant for those convicts whose executions were not registered I had to go through years of old newspapers for the information that I required.

I have included old letters to the Lord Mayor of London with reference to hanging - 500 per year in London itself.

Another interesting trial which was in 1739 was that of Henry, the Fourth Lord Santry who was tried for murder. I have never came across another case where the prisoner was tried with no expense spared.

In the chapter called capital punishment the list of capital offences are included but there was a lot more. I have included my personal remarks against capital punishment on religious grounds. I think I have created more questions than answers but then capital punishment has always been a debatable subject.

This is a short introduction to Belfast Gaol or Antrim Gaol as it was called at its commencement. I have included quite a lot of references which are for the individual who wants to do more in-depth research it has taken me years to gather the following information but I have enjoyed the challenge.

In the town book of Belfast 1613 - 1816. Historical Notices of Old Belfast and its Vicinity by R.M. Young. We read :- "1845 County Gaol completed" 1850 Assizes removed from Carrickfergus to Belfast.

From here we trace our steps backwards into history to ascertain what happened to law breakers prior to the opening of Belfast Prison. "As I Roved Out" by Cathal O'Byrne gives us a picture of those early times. Page 130 reads .... in the year 1772 a general Act was passed being the 11th an 12th Geo.111. Cap.30 entitled : An Act for badging such poor as shall be found unable to support themselves by labour and industry by begging.

Some years after the passing of this act, the corporation of the town advised that the sovereign, accompanied by members of the committee, will occasionally go through the streets in the town for the purpose of 'banishing all strolling beggars.' It was also decided that the black hole be prepared for 'the reception of such strolling beggar as are sent up by the sovereign.' (I'm not quite sure who the sovereign was. He could have been the Lord Mayor or maybe the Sheriff)

In an article on the history of Londonderry's penal institutions, bandbeggars were described as the sturdy fellows. Beggars themselves, they were sent out with staves and cloaks to apprehend the poor unfortunates who went about the streets begging. All strolling beggars were directed forthwith to leave the town and return to their former places of abode. Otherwise they were dealt with according to the rigours of the law. A lock-up which was known as 'the black hole' was set up in Rosemary Street completely prepared for the reception of all persons who may be found to merit such lodgings. From the information available we learn that 'the black hole' had an apartment for men and another for women. Each had a small window with heavy iron bars and other means of illumination. There was a jailor's room convenient and a large apartment for the use of the sovereign or any other magistrate who wished to examine the prisoner. The 'black hole' was used only as a place of temporary confinement for those arrested daily or nightly in the streets and brought before the magistrate the next day. Carrickfergus Gaol was the place for those who were to be detained in custody longer.

From 'A History of Belfast" by George Benn, covering from the earliest times to the close of the 18th century, we read of the next stage of penal institutions - The 'House of Correction.' There was a general complaint in the town about this time that there was no suitable place of confinement for culprits whereby many escaped and caused much inconvenience. Money had been subscribed by the grand jury for this purpose since 1803 and it was probably at this period that the 'House of Correction' at the end of Howard Street, which was then in the fields, was built. It was said to have had a legend cut in stone in prominent letters above the main entrance : 'Within Amend. Without Beware.'

In later times, the house of correction was presided over by two resident magistrates, named respectively O'Donnell and Orme. These two magistrates struck terror into the hearts of all evil doers, and who rarely, if ever, were known to temper their justice with mercy. The 'House of Correction' was built in 1817 and did duty until the erection of the new jail on the Crumlin Road.

On page 109 of The History of Carrickfergus by Miskimmin we read the following paragraph : 1845 July 9th After the Conclusion of the Assizes, Justices Perrin and Ball, having arrived in Belfast from Carrickfergus, entered the new penitentiary, Crumlin Road, Belfast. Accompanied by some members of the grand jury, they inspected every portion of the spacious buildings and the arrangements made for carrying out of the separate system, while the health, the moral and the physical training of the prisoners were properly attended to. After a minute survey, their lordships expressed their perfect satisfaction with the entire arrangements.

The penitentiary was now ready for the reception of prisoners. Those now confined in the House of Correction, including a number of those convicted at the last sessions of Ballymoney and Ballymena, were to be transferred immediately. The prisoners in Carrickfergus were not removed to Belfast until 1850 When under a new act 84 were removed from that establishment on September 1st, 35 of whom were convicts.

The Belfast Directory 1852 reads: 'The new jail stands on an elevated and healthy situation on the Crumlin Road on an area of 10 acres. Designed after the model of Pentonville, near London, the central portion consists of board, reception and waiting rooms, the Governor's department, the chapel and inspection. From the central hall, four wings diverge ; two for males with three-storey ranges and a like number for females. The church was divided into compartments which admit 384 prisoners. The management of the jail was under a board of superintendence and the officers connected therewith were those of an inspector, three chaplains, a surgeon an apothecary an a resident governor.

The Belfast Directory of 1889 mentions the underground passage connected between the court house and the prison and goes on to say 'there are cells for 528 prisoners besides a department for debtors. The building is exceedingly massive and the site one of the most beautiful in Belfast. The discipline strict ; the silent, separate system being closely followed at the time.'

For some information about the cost, the building and the architect, I quote the following source : Belfast Evening Telegraph, Tuesday 27th 1960. - 'Belfast Prison cost £60,000 to build.' In the Belfast Evening Telegraph again on Tuesday, February 25th, 1958 - 'Belfast Prison was built by Messrs. Williams and Scott of Talbot Street, Dublin. The Clerk of Works was Abraham Fitzgibbon of Kilmarnock, County Limerick and Leonard Williams was the driving power on the job.' The famous Belfast architect, Sir Charles Lanyon, was the architect of the prison. He was the son of John Jenkinson Lanyon, a gentleman of Cornish extraction. About 1830 he became an articled pupil in the office of Jack Owen in Dublin. Later he was appointed County Surveyor for Kildare and was soon afterwards transferred at his own request to County Antrim where we find him located at No.2 Donegall Square West. On May 28th 1834, he was appointed County Surveyor for County Antrim during which time he devoted the early part of his career to engineering. Among his first works were the construction of the Coast Road from Larne to Cushendall and the plans for the Queen's Bridge and the Ormeau Bridge in Belfast. He was the engineer in charge of the laying of railway lines from Belfast to Ballymena, Larne and Bangor. The important public buildings for which he was the architect were, Queen's University, the Court House and the County Gaol on Belfast's Crumlin Road, the Custom's House and the Home for the Deaf Dumb and Blind on Belfast's Lisburn Road. He was the pioneer here in the North of Ireland of gothic revival architecture, which is the style of nearly all his work. One of the best examples of his ecclesiastical design is Carlisle Memorial Church in Belfast. A man with a zealous public spirit, he was erected Mayor of Belfast for a number of years and was elected to represent one of the town's constituencies at Westminster in 1862. In the same year he became president of the Royal Institute of Architects in Ireland, an office which he held until 1868 when he was knighted for his many services in this country by the Duke of Abercorn, The Lord Lieutenant. After a long illness he died at home in Whiteabbey in May 1889 and he was buried at Knockbreda.

Other references to Belfast Prison may be found in the Belfast and Ulster Directory 1858, 1859, 1870 and 1880. The following information I have taken from old memos and circulars :- In February 1925, there was a directive by the Minister of Home Affairs, Northern Ireland. As the motor van only conveys female prisoners to Armagh on Mondays, Wednesdays and Saturdays, the female prisoners convicted at Belfast Petty Sessions on Tuesdays Thursdays and Fridays, will be kept in the charge of female searchers in the Block House, Belfast Prison. The Block House was to the right as you came through the front gate of the Prison and was situated in the corner close to the Mater Hospital. I was in the Block House some years ago and from what I can remember, the walls were made of concrete. There were no windows and contained within these walls was a small kitchen, a cell and an officers room.

On March 13th 1925, according to a letter to the Governor refers to the committal of a female prisoner by a Sheriff to Belfast Prison. It goes o to say, 'I am to point out that under orders issued by the Lord Lieutenant dated 9th December 1919 and 10th April 1920, Armagh Prison is the only prison in Northern Ireland to which females, so arrested, should be committed. The Governor was instructed to remove the prisoner to Armagh under escort straight away.' This was the last reference to a female prisoner being held in Belfast Prison.

From a Ministerial minutes sheet dated September 3rd 1925 we find that the Ministry of Home Affairs sanctioned the building of a block of 16 houses on the ground to the west of the front gate at a total cost of £8,550.

In a circular dated 6th January 1926, which implies that the following people lived in the houses; the medical Officer, Governor, Deputy Governor, Chief Warder and Matron. Their quarters were to be accordingly :- The exterior woodwork of the cottages 'dark green', the interior woodwork, such as, doors, windows, architraves, skirtings, stair railings etc. will be painted purple or dark brown. Some range of colours! If you think that is bad I shall quote from a circular from Dublin Castle, dated May 23rd 1890 - The cell doors shall be painted purple or brown, the architrave ultramarine blue mixed with a very little blue black, iron work, gallery rails etc. black. Still on the subject of painting, a minutes sheet from the Ministry of Finance dated August 21st 1925, painting of the walls of the several wards of the prison instead of the present practice of whitewashing : walls should be painted a suitable colour to a height of 5 feet from the floor. The doors and the frame-work should also be painted. The installation of sinks in each ward for emptying slops was a real breakthrough. I came across an old circular for the houses at Mountjoy Gaol which stated : A cart from the Gaol will come around every third day to collect ashes and your buckets with ashes and slops. In my view it meant body waste as they had no flush toilets in those days. I would presume it would have been the same for the gaols in general.

There were rules relating to anyone who occupied the prison cottages. I shall relate to a few.

1. Nails or pegs should not b put into the walls or woodwork under no pretext.

2. No cattle, goats, dogs fowl, rabbits or pigeons were allowed on the premises.

3. Although the people of the cottages got free water and gas, it was stressed that if they used too much water, a meter would be fitted to their supply and charge accordingly. The gas had to be turned off at 10.30 pm. each night.

4. No officer who has children over 17 years of age living with him will be allowed to live in the cottages.

Capital Punishment - Hanging

For many centuries in Ireland the normal method of carrying out sentence of death on capital felons was hanging. There were other methods, it is true, but none claimed as many victims. In the Middle ages every town and abbey and almost all the more important English and Irish lords were entitled to carry out hangings. Gallows were almost ubiquitous and are commemorated in street and placenames. In my own hometown of Dromore, County Down, the name Gallows Street serves as a reminder of what went on at the top of the hill where the road forks. Carrickfergus in County Antrim has a replica of the so-called 'three sisters': three 5m high posts, driven into the ground, forming a triangle with header beams, over which the hangman slung his rope, running from post to post. In Newtownards, County Down, at the junction of the old and new Portaferry Roads, is hangman's Hill. These towns retained their gallows until the late nineteenth century.

Abbots and lords were loath to surrender their right to carry out hangings for various reasons. One motive was greed ; the chattels of the condemned man passed to them.

During the reign of Edward I little regard was paid to human life, and this is reflected in the amount of executions carried out. In the year 1279, for instance, no fewer than 280 Jews were hanged for 'clipping' coins. This was a common offence and many paid for it with their lives. Coin-clippers fared no better under Henry VIII, who reigned for more than 37 years. Stow records that 72,000 executions took place while he was on the throne. This average of 2,000 executions a year declined slightly under Elizabeth I. By the beginning of the nineteenth century the number of capital offences - which included stealing a handkerchief, shooting a rabbit and adopting a disguise - in the Statute Book had risen to 222. This rise is attributable to the increasing emphasis on the value of property. The following list of capital offences is taken, in turn, from the list drawn up by the abolitionist P. Colquoun LL.D. and published in Basil Montagu's 'Opinions of Different Authors upon the Punishment of Death':

arson, or wilfully and maliciously burning a house, barns with corn etc;

attempting to kill Privy Councillors etc;

bankrupts not surrendering, or concealing their effects;

11

being an accessory to felonies deemed capital;

breaking down the head of a fish-pond, whereby fish may be lost (so-called 'Black Act');

burglary or house-breaking in the night-time;

challenging jurors above 20 in capital felonies;

standing mute, concealing the death of a bastard child;

cutting down trees in an avenue, garden etc;

cutting down river or sea-banks;

cutting hop-binds;

destroying ships, or setting them on fire;

destroying silk or velvet in the loom, or the tools for manufacturing thereof, or destroying woollen goods, racks or tools, or entering a house for that purpose;

deer-stealing (second offence, although under certain circumstances sometimes for a first offence);

destroying turnpikes or bridges, gates, weighing-engines, locks, sluices, engines for draining marshes etc;

escape from prison in certain cases;

forgery of deeds, bonds, bills, notes, public securities, warrants etc;

embezzlement;

burning or causing damage to dockyards;

highway robbery (in certain cases);

housebreaking in the daytime;

maiming or killing cattle maliciously;

maliciously maiming or disfiguring any person, or lying in wait for this purpose;

mutiny, desertion etc, by martial or statute law;

murder;

impersonating bail, acknowledging fines or judgments in another's name;

piracy, or robbing ships and vessels at sea;

forcibly hindering the captain of one's ship from fighting;

committing perjury while a prisoner under Insolvency Acts;

privately stealing or picking pockets (sum stolen must exceed one shilling);

pulling down houses, churches etc;

rape or the forcible violation of chastity;

returning from transportation, or being at large in the kingdom after sentencing;

riots by 12 or more persons and not dispersing in an hour after

12

proclamation;

robbery of the mail;

sacrilege;

setting fire to coal-mines;

purloining one's master's goods (value of goods must exceed 40 shillings);

sending threatening letters;

shooting at a revenue officer or at any other person;

shoplifting (goods valued at more than 5 shillings);

smuggling by persons armed, or assembling arms for that purpose;

sodomy, a crime against nature, committed with either man or beast;

enlisting into armies or navies of foreign countries;

stealing an heiress;

stealing bonds, bills, banknotes;

stealing banknotes or bills from letters;

stealing above 40 shillings in any house;

stealing above 40 shillings on a river;

stealing linen etc. from bleaching grounds, or destroying linen therein;

stealing horses cattle or sheep;

stabbing a person unarmed or not having a weapon drawn if he die within six months;

stealing woollen cloths from tenter grounds;

stealing from a ship in distress;

taking a reward for helping another to stolen goods (in certain cases);

treason and petty treason etc;

counterfeiting gold and silver coin etc;

counterfeit money (third offence).

Once the judge had announced, 'You shall be taken to a place of execution where you shall suffer death by hanging', the prisoner had to come to terms with the fact that he had a date with the hangman. Being on 'Death Row', during his period of appeal, which could take months, could change a man. Some turned to religion, reconciling themselves to the consequences of their crimes.

Three pairs of prison officers assigned to the condemned man worked eight-hour shifts. These officers stayed with the man until his execution. Often close relationships developed between officer and prisoner as they spent months waiting, talking and playing games. But the officer's permanent presence in the condemned cell

- they were locked in with the prisoner - was not designed for purposes of entertainment; true, they provided a distraction or company for the condemned man, but their job was to prevent their charge from cheating the hangman's noose. Hermann Goering, Hitler's crony, poisoned himself shortly before he was due to be hanged following his conviction at the Nuremberg Trials. It is common for condemned men to try to devise ways of taking their own life rather than be hanged. 'There was no way I could have done it,' one has said, 'If there was a way, many would have done it.'

A prison cook was charges with preparing and tasting the condemned man's food. This was to ensure he, the condemned man, did not cheat the hangman by poisoning himself. The officer looked upon his task as another 'occupational hazard'.

The Governor of the prison and the prison doctor saw the prisoner at least once a day. The chaplain also visited the condemned man once a day, if requested. The condemned man would bathe and exercise when the other prisoners were locked up, between 1200 and 1400 hours and then between 1600 and 1730 hours. He was allowed visits once a week or more often at the Governor's discretion. He was also allowed to write to family and friends and could request reading material. When the day of execution was approaching the prisoner was told to expect visits from friends and relatives. At the meeting the condemned man was given a hint that he had barely 18 hours to live.

Many have called death by hanging, inhuman and barbaric. They have said that no-one has the right to take another's life. But death by hanging is much quicker than death by, say, gassing or electrocution; it takes only 4 seconds. In the time it has taken you to read this paragraph a man could have died by hanging.

Albert Pierrepoint, perhaps Ireland's most notorious hangman, who in his career hanged more than 400 people, including women and war criminals described his trade as 'the most humane way to put a man to death.'

Contrary to popular opinion, a man sentenced to death by hanging does not die of strangulation, but of breaking of the third cervical vertebra ('the odontoid process'). In his book, Pierrepoint, whose father and uncle were also hangmen, claims never to have seen a man suffer on the rope. The drop, Pierrepoint explains, is calculated in proportion to his weight, so that the man suffers for less than four seconds.

The execution itself was carried out by an experienced officer, although several others were involved in the planning beforehand. To ensure that the hanging was carried out without a hitch, the hangman and his assistant tested the trap-door the day before the execution. The condemned man was traditionally only told of the date and the time of the execution on being taken back to his cell after his family and friends had seen him for the last time.

The warrant of sentence was read out by the Governor to the condemned man, usually after lunch. At this meeting the man is also asked what he would like for his last meal and if he would like to see his minister or priest.

For a man with less than 10 hours to live, sleep does not come easily. This was the hardest time for the prisoner and prison officers alike. Old hands tell me that a prison does not sleep the night before a hanging. Just before dawn the sound of the opening of the doors on 'Death Row' signalled that death was less than a minute away.

The prisoner was then led to the hangman's cell, usually next door. His legs were strapped together and his arms were strapped to his side. He was asked if he would like to pray with his minister or priest and, more often than not, availed himself of this opportunity. He had no indication of when the trap-door would open. As he arose from his knees, a hood was placed over his head and a noose around his neck. As the hangman put his hand on his shoulder, the lever is pushed. The man felt his legs in the air and knew that death was a few seconds away.

Hangings were witnessed by a magistrate, a doctor, the Governor of the prison and a cleric.

Afterwards the rope was lowered and the doctor certified that the man was clinically dead. Once this was done, the remains were buried within the prison grounds. Finally, a notice, proclaiming the execution of the death sentence, as pinned to the prison gates for public consumption.

The whole concept of capital punishment down through the years was always a bowl of contention. In compiling this book on hangings, after 11 years research and after being a prison officer for 20 years and during that time having worked with some of the worst types of prisoners, I must ask myself if I believe in capital punishment? And if so, would I be willing to push the lever which operates the trap-door on which the condemned person stands with a noose around his neck and a hood over his face? I don't honestly think I could.

I remember listening to a group of young prisoners talking about a person whom the individual had murdered. He said with shark cold eyes, "he cried like a child and before he was killed outright he was crying for his mammy." Such evil I have come across a few times. The following views which were expressed in a series of letters to the Lord Mayor of London, give us a little insight into capital punishment in their day.

In 1786 when men were condemned to die - and they were brought to a situation the most dreadful, when all the world deserted them, and nothing is left but an ignominion, an untimely and perhaps a painful death, when, at the hour of appearance before that Being whose judgment shall stand forever - what is the frame of their minds? A cool indifference, or a fixed stupidity, the mixture of ignorance and insensibility - nay, some triumphantly boast of their situation and end their day in which they call heroic courage, that is the madness of despair. To such men, what is the punishment of hanging? Nothing, it is merely the mean to prevent them from doing any more mischief, but it strikes no terror, produces no penitence, and its effect on the living are not less futile, an execution is a kind of holiday to the idle thief, and he practices his art under the gallows feet. But whatever the effects of our numerous executions may be on the objects, the effect on society in general are deplorable; on a moderate computation, five-hundred men and women are hanged in year, and we may safely conclude that five-thousand more are ready and deserving of the same punishment, when their time comes. He went on to say, It has been tried to execute them in great numbers, but which purpose has this answered, there are twenty more, nay double, and triple that number, there are fifty's and sixty's ready for the same punishment, and actually under the same sentence. As every object becomes from its frequency, so the frequency of executions destroys all the impressions of horror with which they were once attended and to excite they were dreaded. The hardened and insensible villain are as indifferent about dying by the rope as if they died in their beds.

The author of another letter to the Lord Mayor of London in 1786, whose name is omitted, goes on to say,

My main object was to point out the cause of the increase of thieves, by which name I mean fellows of every degree. The number of low ale houses where money at times is wasted in the worst of company, and to the destruction of reason and principle.

The number of bad women who mix with the men, and seduce them into every species of daring wickedness.

His observations were divided into three headings:-

1. The general profligacy of the times.
2. The increase of public amusements.
3. The promiscuous intercourse of all criminals while in prison.

1. The General Profligacy of The Times

This is usually an object of ridicule with the men of the world, who are content to believe, that we are no worse than any who have gone before us. Was there ever a time when executions were so frequent? Was there ever a time when the seduction of females was more common and less abhorred? Was there ever a time when gambling prevailed in a greater degree? Are not half of our noble families ruined by gaming? Was there ever a time when divorces were more frequent? And was there ever such a time when less attention was paid to the religion of the country, to the laws of morality of sobriety and decorum? I aver that the profligacy of the present time is unprecedented in the history of Great Britain, however we may find something like it in the declining days of Rome. (This was written in 1786)

2. The Increase of Public Amusements

There is usually a very wise argument used in the defence of public amusements. The people must have them. And why must they have them? Because the little time they have spared from labour must never be employed in cultivating their minds, promoting health and cheerfulness by the comfort of a family fireside; and because sobriety and temperance are not consistent with idleness and extravagance that we have at present.

The pernicious effects of many places of amusements, fitted for the taste of the lower classes, appear from the amazing sums of money collected at such places, the bulk of the lower classes money goes on strollers and vagabonds.

He goes on to say, "The frequency of executions, therefore causes which have been enumerated. If there were any good served by this;

17

if it really lessened the number of thieves; if it worked penitence in the surviving, and drove them from their wickedness; if it was an object of terror, or considered really as punishment, no remonstrance would be offered against it. But the reverse is the truth it serves no good purpose; it lessens not the number of criminals, who every day increase in number.

It works not penitence in the surviving, nor inclines them to leave wickedness in which they are hardened; it is not an object of terror even to the immediate who rob and steal, in the awful moment of their fellow creature, perhaps their associates, being launched into eternity.

Some have blamed the leniency of the throne, "Many, they say, are pardoned, and it were better to hang all, without mercy". What would we gain by this? Instead of 500 we should have occasion to hang perhaps 5000 in the kingdom in one year - blessed circumstance in the history of England! We might then indeed justly be considered as madmen, as fools, as cruel in the extreme; and what is worse, even this massacre, if I may use the expression, would leave us just where we were, five-thousand more would be ready against the next Assizes.

My Views on the Continued Abolition of Capital Punishment from a Christian Standpoint

I am aware that mine is but a feeble voice raised in support of the continued abolition of capital punishment. My views are based on the Scriptures and on the principles of Christianity.

If murder is to be punished by death, then, I feel, a better - if one can use this adjective in this context - method of taking life must be found. Although some make use of the scriptural argument to justify their support for capital punishment, it is my opinion that the well-known passage beginning 'Whoso shedeth....' should be considered not a command but a prediction. It should be interpreted thus: kill not, for you will meet the same doom at another's hand. It is true that murder is, in other places, commanded to be punished by death, but we do not live under the Mosaic Dispensation: no-one is killed nowadays for gathering sticks on a Sunday. The spirit of the New Testament is certainly against capital punishment; in it one finds no command for the taking away of a murderer' life.

Execution of sentence of death within a fixed time after conviction is most cruel. It may at first seem merciful, but upon examination of this procedure one is forced to admit that it is in fact not a mercy that a man should know in advance the date of his death. Executions must be carried out within thirty days.

People murder as a result of some powerful operative cause, from some motive, be it revenge, lust, covetousness, jealousy or in hot blood. But the law does not act in hot blood. It carries out its dread sentence in a most cool manner, long after the heat of the moment in which the crime was committed and long after the crime has been forgotten by most of those not directly involved.

If one life has already been taken, what is the use of taking another? The law purports to show its respect for life by strangling those who show none. If the murderer could only be confined or imprisoned, so that he could kill no more, then the law would really be showing respect for life.

If the murderer is not fit for this world, is he fit for the next? If there be no eternity, if our longing for immortality be foolish and vain, then the culprit's life might be taken away. But, if, on the other hand, eternity exists, then is it not a shame, is it not cruel, to hurry a man who is not fit for this sinful world into the presence of a Holy God?

But the law must be carried out. Yes, the law! If, however, the Gospel had thoroughly permeated society, then the law might have been different. Does it not seem a shame that we can do no better with a murderer than suspend him between Heaven and earth?

The main reason why public executions were abolished was because it was felt that they were injurious to morals and favoured the devil, so it was decided to have private executions instead. I believe that if ministers and doctors, whose duty it was to preserve life and not to take it or see it taken away but who attended executions in their official capacity, had stayed away, it would have hastened the end of capital punishment much more speedily.

When the death penalty was finally abolished, we saw an end also to the wretched practice of petitioning the monarch or the Lord Lieutenant, who despite their exalted secular status, had no right to be exalted into gods. Is there not something appalling about the practice of calmly and deliberately putting to death by hanging a fellow human-being, whatever his crime, if he profess deep repentance? And who would not repent faced with the terrible reality of the gallows? It is against the spirit of Christianity, demoralises society, And is an affront to the mercies of the Almighty. Let us hope that capital punishment remains abolished in this country and that it be abolished elsewhere.

Few things in life are black and white; there are always arguments for and against. In the light of this, the following comments from a condemned man on the gallows are worthy of some consideration. As was customary at public executions, the man was given the opportunity to make a speech. Most men just stated that they guilty or innocent. An admission of guilt appears to have relieved the hangman's conscience. But this particular man who was about to be executed in Wicklow in 1738 appears, from his long and in-depth knowledge of world history, to have been quite learned. What he said was this:

My friends, you assemble to see - what? A man leap into the abyss of death! Look and you will see me go with as much courage as ....when he leapt into the gulf to save his country from destruction. What will you say of me? You say that no man without virtue can be courageous! You see what I am - I'm a little fellow.

What is the difference between running into a poor man's debt .... and clipping a pistol to a man's breast and taking from him his purse? Yet the one shall thereby obtain a coach and honour and

20

titles, the other what? A cart and a rope.

Don't imagine from this that I am hardened. I acknowledge the just judgment of God has overtaken me. My redeemer knows that murder was far from my heart and what I did was through rage and passion, being provoked by the deceased.

Take warning comrades. Think what would I now give that I had lived another life. Courageous? You'll say I've killed a man. Marlborough killed his thousands, and Alexander and many others who would have done the like are famous in history for great men. Oye, that's the case, one solitary man. I'm a little murderer and must be hanged.

Marlborough and Alexander plundered countries; they were great men. I ran into debt with the ale-wife; I must be hanged.

How many men were lost in Italy and upon the Rhine during the last war for settling a king in Poland? Both sides could not be in the right! They are great men; but I killed a solitary man.

The Execution of Robert O'Neill, Aged 18, Soldier. on 21st June 1854

On the 22nd August 1853 in one of the common rooms of the Belfast Infantry Barracks, Private Robert Henry O'Neill murdered Corporal Robert Brown. Both were members of the 1st Battalion of the 12th (East Worchester) Regiment of Foot.

It appears Corporal Brown put Private O'Neill on report for a minor misconduct but when Corporal Brown was sitting at a table in the barrack room, Private O'Neill deliberately raised his musket and fired at the corporal which resulted in his death. As O'Neill tried to flee from the scene, he was arrested. The following day a verdict was brought against him by a coroner's jury.

His trial was held at the Spring Assizes for County Antrim before Mr. Sergeant Howley and the result was that he was ordered for execution on 5th May 1854, before the Judges of the Queen's Bench, Dublin. It was reported at the time, and indeed in most trials when a judge had to sentence a prisoner to execution, that when the judge donned the black cap and began to pass the death sentence tears began to fall down his face. O'Neill had to be supported by warders in the dock. Afterwards, convict O'Neill was transferred back to the condemned cell (No. 3 in 'D' Wing). I have stood in this cell and tried to picture how he felt.

Three priests visited him while he was in the death cell. They were Messrs., McCartan, Martin and Fagan. On the morning of the execution he requested to be executed in his military dress uniform. He stated that he would feel uncomfortable appearing before the crowd in his grave clothes. His request was granted.

It was reported at the time that crowds began to assemble at the gaol from early morning but by the time of the execution it was estimated to number around 20,000. The authorities did not expect such a large crowd, but because of its size they decided to dispatch extra troops to the are in case there was any trouble.

It is of general interest to make note of its size. The force consisted of one detachment from each of the depots then stationed in this garrison - the 62nd and 68th under the command of Major Mathias; the D Troop of the 2nd Dragoons (Queen's Grays); 110 of the County Antrim Constabulary and 30 of the County Down Constabulary, under the command of Captain Flinter, County Inspector and Sub-

Inspectors Daly, Henry and Holmes of the County Antrim and Williams of the County Down.

The infantry soldiers were posted inside the railings of the prison, (the cottages were not built at this stage) and the dragoons and part of the constabulary were on the road in front of the gaol for some distance on either side. The remainder of the constabulary were positioned on the forecourt of the Court-house opposite the gaol. All in all, a total of 940 sabres and bayonets.

H.M.P. Belfast had been built on the model of Millbank and Pentonville prisons. It had no scaffold. This was no oversight on the architects's part for H.M.P. Belfast had not originally been intended for use as a county prison; at the time of its construction Carrickfergus was Antrim's Assize town and its prison served the county. Thus the scaffold used for O'Neill's execution was a temporary affair. It had been erected in front of one of the windows to the left of the main steps which led into the main hallway. He was led to the ladder which took him unto the scaffold and once he arrived there, the hood was placed over his head followed soon after by the dreaded noose. The public in general would have had trouble seeing him as the main gate would have been closed. The outer wall which ran the full length in front of the prison would have been half the height it is now, as it was not raised till a later date. This meant the public could only see part of the scaffold from further up the Crumlin Road or by positioning themselves further down the road.

The hangman, although his face was covered by a hood, was himself a prisoner at Belfast Gaol. He had been sentenced to a term of imprisonment because of an assault charge.

O'Neill appeared on the scaffold and his prayers, along with those of the clergy, could be heard by the motionless crowd. They also heard the swing of the trap door. The death itself was described as instantaneous but it did not stop a scream coming from the women in the crowd. Shortly afterwards the crowd dispersed.

The Ballyleeson Murder
The Execution of Daniel Ward, 8th April 1863

On the evening of Friday 9th May 1862, Daniel Ward called at the house of William Wright, where his friend Charles Wilgar stayed, and asked if Wilgar would be going home that night; when he was told that Wilgar had no such plans, Ward said he would wait for him. When Wilgar arrived, the two friends and travelling companions had tea together and chatted. Before Ward took his leave, he had ascertained that Wilgar would be going home the following Saturday evening.

Next evening, Ward called again at Wright's and waited for Wilgar to return from work. As on the previous evening, they had tea together ..... for what Ward had already decided would be the last time. At 6pm. the two men set off for Wilgar's father's.

Wilgar was never seen alive again. His body was recovered from the River again the following Tuesday. He had been beaten badly about the head. It later transpired that Wilgar's head wounds had been caused by some heavy object; his skull was shattered. Later it emerged that a 4lb stone, tied up in the corner of a handkerchief and found in the river near the body, had been the murder weapon. It also emerged that the handkerchief belonged to Ward and been given to him some time before by one o the witnesses who testified against him at his trial.

At the trial Ward, described as an ignorant, illiterate man who had neglected his education from his earliest childhood, was found by the jury to be guilty without any recommendations of mercy - within an hour. Baron easy was judge, and his passing of the death sentence on Ward appeared to upset him and the prisoner's relations far more than it did Ward himself, who according to newspaper reports was 'indifferent to the whole procedure.'

When the Deputy Clerk of the Crown told Ward that he had been, in due form of the law, arraigned, indicted, tried and convicted of the murder of Charles Wilgar, and asked him if he had anything to say as to why sentence of death and execution according to law should not be passed upon him Ward replied that he was not guilty. The judge replied at length:

'Daniel Ward, I have heard with regret and pain that last observation which has just fallen from you. The protestation of innocence is of no avail after the verdict of twelve men upon their oaths. It cannot be listened to by the judge, and it cannot be attended to by the government. After a most careful and patient investigation of your case, in which you had the benefit of all that professional zeal and ability could do for you, a jury of twelve impartial, sensible men have pronounced upon their oaths that you are guilty of the crime with which you have been charged, and in the propriety of that judgment I am bound to say in justice to them - more especially after the protestation that you have made - that I fully concur in it.

Although no witness was produced who saw you do the fatal deed, yet the Crown has been enabled to lay before the jury and before me, evidence of facts which in their judgment and mine have established your guilt. It now only remains for me to pronounce the sentence which the law awards as the consequence of your crime and its conviction. You have taken the life of a fellow creature, and for that life your life is forfeited. He, the victim of your crime, was hurled into eternity before his very thought could pray. Time shall be afforded you for preparation, for repentance, and for prayer.

In common with all who have heard this case, I entertain feelings of deep compassion for those unhappy beings to whom reference has been made, who are connected to you by the nearest and dearest ties of blood and affection, who, though innocent of your great crime, are involved in the fatal consequences of it and must long deplore your untimely and ignominious death. But the feelings can in no way interfere with the performance of my duty, which, though painful, is imperative, which the law has imposed on me, and that duty is to pronounce the sentence of the law which dooms and consigns you to an ignominious death upon the scaffold. Time, as I said, shall be allowed you to prepare for that dreadful fate; and I pray you t devote to repentance the interval which I shall allow to elapse between the pronouncing of death and execution of that sentence. Employ I beseech you, the last few days that remain to you on this earth in repentance and in prayer - deep, sincere, heartfelt repentance for the crime you have committed, and for other ills done in the flesh, and in earnest supplication for that forgiveness and that mercy of which all have need, and which are denied to none. Ask and it will e afforded to you, the assistance and the spiritual comfort of the minister of whatever church you belong to. Listen to their exhortations. They will necessarily and naturally bear more weight with you than any other words which fall from me. But do not neglect to attend to their words.

It only remains for me to terminate this painful scene by pronouncing in formal terms that sentence which the law requires the judge to pronounce, and requires the ministers of justice to carry into effect.

And (putting on the black cap and becoming very affected) that sentence is that you, Daniel Ward, be taken from the dock in which you now stand to the jail in which you have been hitherto contained, and that from thence you be taken, on Wednesday, the eighth day of April 1863, to the public place of execution, and be there hanged by the neck until you are dead, and that your body be buried within the precincts of the jail in which you have been last confined previous to your conviction, and may the great God whom you have offended have mercy on your immortal soul.

The prisoner bowed to the judge, and left the dock in the company of two jailers; he seemed the most unconcerned man in court that day, for he reacted with such unconcern that he ate his dinner in a few minutes afterwards.

The reader can read for himself the lengthy and very detailed reports on all the court proceedings in copies of the Northern Whig from this period.

On the day of execution an immense crowd of some several thousands had gathered on the Crumlin Road and i the fields bordering it. Every available vantage point was taken up by those come to witness the execution. Most of those present were lower-working-class and, regrettably, many were female. They revelled in the preparations for the disgusting spectacle. Rain began to fall in a gentle shower shortly before 8am, but it had no effect on the crowd which stayed put.

In the surrounding fields off the Crumlin Road, in which Belfast Jail stands to this day, a disorderly rabble amused themselves by misbehaving, pitching anyone unfortunate enough to get in their way, into the road; they seemed not in the slightest awed by the ongoing preparations for the forthcoming grisly spectacle.

Twice the grim death-passage was opened up, but only to allow the executioner to finalise the arrangements for the hanging.

After a fourteen minute delay, during which time tension rose, the wretched prisoner Ward kept his appointment on the scaffold, white cap drawn over his face. The vast crowd lapsed into momentary silence as Ward took up position over the trap-door. Many eyes were averted from him. Ward himself, though bound, twice turned towards Belfast, as if with a lingering fondness, as the hangman tidied up a few loose ends.

Another shorter pause then ensued. The eyes of the crowd still fixed upon the scaffold drank in the victim, the drop, the rope, the iron bar above. Time seemed to drag its heels, then the bolt was pulled, and the figure of Ward dropped, the rope tightened into a rigid line, and the quivering body swung round, mocking life. Ward had been consigned to eternity without a struggle.

The public, and the jury, will have been satisfied to learn that Ward did not continue to profess his 'innocence' right to the very end, but finally came clean and had the honesty to confess to his great crime. His confession was made some time prior to his execution, but, as long as there was hope, it was not made public. It ran thus:

" I, Daniel Ward, now a prisoner in the County Antrim Jail, Belfast, and under the sentence of death for the murder of Charles Wilgar, on the 10th of May last, in the presence of Almighty God, before whom I must soon stand, do make the following confession, and declare every portion of it to be strictly true :-

On the evening of the 9th May I was in Belfast seeking for employment at any work I could obtain, but not did not succeed. I left Belfast between four and five o'clock in the evening, and, during my walk home, I thought of (as the last remedy) robbing or murdering some one in order to get money. My mind did not settle at that time on any one in particular but I felt no act whatever would prevent me from obtaining it. Before reaching home, I called at William Wright's to ask him if he could give me a job, for I was idle. So far as to murdering Charles Wilgar in particular had not taken possession of my mind, nor any other if I could get money any other way.

On the next morning May the 10th, I went to Belfast. On going, I sat upon a heap of stones, thinking what to do; I took up a stone, and put it into my pocket handkerchief. I left Belfast between three or four that evening. On this evening also, I went to William Wright's and waited till Wright and Wilgar returned from work.

My object in waiting in Wright's was till it was dusk, that I might obtain by some means what I wanted, and had not up till this time settled my mind in taking the life of Charles Wilgar. After tea in Wright's, I started with Charles Wilgar, towards home, and I do not think it was five minutes before the act that I determined to take his watch or life. I knew he had a watch. We came to a narrow path - he went before me. I took then the stone which was in my handkerchief out of my pocket and gave him a blow. He fell, but did not speak. He was rising, I think, on his hands and feet. I then gave him a second blow - took his watch from him and put him in the water. The plunge appeared to revive him, for I saw him swimming across the Lagan, and thought he would get out at the other side. I then threw the stone and the handkerchief into the water, and went to Lisburn and pawned the watch for two pounds - and when on Monday evening I heard he was missing, I knew he was drowned. I also solemnly declare before God, that I never injured so as to take away the life of any other man, woman or child.

I know and feel I am a great sinner in the sight of God. My past life has been an unprofitable one; happiness was the great object of my life, but I feel now what a bad way I took to obtain it.

My short life may be said to have been a prayerless one, for although I did at times go through the form, I see now that it was no prayer at all. My sabbaths were badly spent, and the things of an endless life seldom or ever took possession of my mind. I thank God that for his namesake He has brought me to think of Him. The last four months have been the happiest days of my life. I have no enmity against a creature living. I willingly forgive all, and ask them to forgive me. I entreat all of my relatives and friends to live for eternity ; it is the only thing which will make them happy.

I have cast myself for salvation on the atoning blood of Jesus Christ. I believe that he will fulfil His own promise, that whoever cometh to Him with a heart truly sorry for the past and trusting in the Saviour will not be cast away. I have nothing of myself, and deserve nothing but His wrath. I believe He will have mercy on me and receive me. I could wish that all who are living as I did would consider their ways, lest they are brought to an end like mine ; they would obtain more comfort from a single promise of Christ than from the whole world. 'For God so loved men as to give His own son to die for them.' 'And He is exalted a Prince and a Saviour, to give to them that ask Him true repentance and pardon.'

I have had a fair trial, and have no fault to find with it. But Jane McCullagh and Rebecca McCullagh's statement, so far as ever having given me a handkerchief, or having had conversation with her in Lisburn on the evening of the 10th May, or having seen her at all on that evening, is untrue. I have no more to add, except to give

my sincere thanks to the chaplain, the Rev. Charles Allen ; the governor, and warders of the prison, for their continued attention and kindness to me during my imprisonment."
DANIEL WARD
County Gaol, Belfast, March, 1863.

Ward's body, having remained suspended for the usual period, was placed in a plain coffin, and the remains were conveyed to a lace of burial within the precincts of the jail, where the remains of the soldier O'Neill had been laid previously. The chaplain, together with the Sheriff, Under-Sheriff, governor of the prison, and warders followed to the grave of the unfortunate man who but one hour beforehand had been full of health and vigour.

And that was the end of one of Ulster's most notorious murderers - a terrible example and awful warning to us all. The fate of Daniel Ward will not soon be forgotten.

The evidence proved clearly that Daniel Ward did not kill in the heat of the moment, but cooly and deliberately. He went to meet his victim carrying with him a weapon he planned to use. He sat down with an unemulated coolness to have tea and smoke with a man he was determined to kill within the space of an hour. There was no motive for the perpetration of this dreadful crime except that of robbery. To gain the price of a paltry watch, Ward was prepared to commit a diabolical crime unparalleled in Ulster's history. On a fine spring evening in May, when Wilgar was returning to gladden his father's home, he was struck down by the hand that should have been extended warmly to him in friendship.

It is to be hoped that it will be a long, long time before Ulster sees the likes of the 'Ballyleeson Murder,' but, then again, how many times have we heard these self same words repeated since, and all to no avail.

The Durham Street Murder
The Execution of John Daly on 27th April 1876

John Daly was executed at H.M.P. Belfast on 27th April 1876 for the murder of Margaret Whitley. He was 40 years old and held a small farm near Dungannon. He had one brother and one sister. His father died when he was young. His brother, who was older than John, died in an accident at a local coal pit.

At the age of 27 John quarrelled with his mother and sister over their land and left for Belfast. He found work there as a labourer in the docks area. Before long he had also met a woman, Mary Ann Whitley, a mill-worker. They married.

On the morning of 15th September 1875, the naked and blood-stained body of a woman was discovered in Bathurst Court off Durham Street. As the day wore on and the news spread like wildfire throughout the city, a little girl called Whiteside identified the body as that of Margaret Whitley, a charwoman, who had lived locally. Margaret Whitley was Mary Ann Daly's aunt. The Dalys lived in Durham Street and Margaret had been seen at their house the previous day. The police were soon at Daly's door. The Dalys were obviously implicated to some degree in the murder of Mrs Whitley; it was up to the R.I.C. o determine to which degree.

It emerged that the deceased had been seen under the influence of drink at the Daly's. John Daly, also under the influence, had been seen there too. Not only had he been seen at home - he had been seen at home lifting a stool and bringing it down on Whitley as she lay on what passed for a bed. This was the last time she had been seen alive. It was also established that Daly's wife and family (a blind infant boy and a 12-year-old girl) had stayed away from home through fear the previous evening. The evidence so far collated pointed at Daly as the murderer and he was arrested. When taken into custody, Daly seemed unaware that anything strange had taken place at his home the previous evening.

When the police examined the Daly household, they found enough evidence to prove that the murder had occurred there. The dwelling was a typical drunkard's hovel. There was hardly any furniture in the two rooms the Dalys occupied. Even the 'bed' was nothing more than straw strewn on the hard floor and covered by an old cloth. It also served as the family couch. Apart from this, the only items of furniture in the room were a table and the stool with which Daly had clobbered Whitley. Blood was found everywhere. There seemed to be little doubt that Daly had done it.

Whitley's body had been covered by a couple of old garments, which were later proved to have belonged to the Daly family. The garments that she had been wearing at the time of the murder were found not far off. They had been placed over a grating; the murderers intention had obviously been to let the blood drip from the clothes into the drain, thus removing evidence. The clothes must have been soaked in blood for Whitley' head, face, and arms were lacerated; the fatal blows, though, had been inflicted on the lower part of the body.

The murder weapon, the stool, had broken into four pieces. Daly's own daughter had seen him wielding it. She was to be the principle witness against her father.

Whitley's young daughter had been told by Daly's daughter that her mother was lying drunk in the house on Durham Street. When the daughter went to see if her mother was still there, at about 8pm on the evening before the body was discovered Daly told her that her mother was not there. A workmate who called for Daly the following morning found him at home and ready for work. Basing its case on this evidence, the prosecution had little difficulty in proving that Daly had been at home all night. Mrs Whitley and her niece, it emerged at the trial, spent a lot of time together. It was not so much family ties that drew them together but a common liking for alcohol. Daly had, in the period preceding the murder, attended work regularly, so regularly indeed, that his workmates looked upon him as a man of steady habits and good character. His wife on the other hand, had unfortunately fallen in with bad company, including that of the unmarried Whitley, and on more than one occasion Daly had had to go looking for his wife at her aunt's. Her husband had frequently put his wife out of the house, but the day before the murder she had sneaked in through the back door when her husband was at work. When he came home unexpectedly early he found her, he hit her and threw her out again, before pawning a clock on the way back to work.

Mother and daughter went to Whitley's and returned to Durham Street with the aunt. The little girl was then sent out to buy drink. Whitley soon began to complain of a headache and lay down on the bed. Before long Daly, who had also been drinking, came home. Mrs

Daly saw her husband before he saw her and fled out of the house. When Daly ordered Whitley - before his daughter - to get up and go, she refused.

It was at this point that Daly attacked Whitley with the stool. His terrified daughter saw this as she hurried out of the house.

Those who came into contact with Daly after his arrest were struck by his apparent indifference to the seriousness of his situation and by his general demeanour. He came across as a man who had not much reason to care about his life, whose misery could not be any greater than it already was.

His trial which lasted two days, began at the Antrim Assizes, before Baron Fitzgerald, on 22nd March 1876. He was found guilty and sentenced to death. Some members of the jury recommended that Daly be shown mercy and a petition was sent to the Lord Lieutenant. After considering the circumstances, the Lord Lieutenant decided that the law must take its course.

Daly was a quiet and orderly prisoner. He displayed humility to his religious advisors, and an earnest desire to join in the spiritual exercises organised by the jail's Roman Catholic chaplain, the Rev. M.Hamill.

Shortly before his execution he was visited by his mother and his wife. They visited separately and did not stay long.

The erection of the scaffold, which had been in progress for about a week, was completed one day early. It was situated at the entrance to the area formerly known as the 'debtors prison', o the northern side of the prison. Oblong-shaped, it had a trap-door in the centre of the platform. This trap-door did not, as was usual at the time, open in two parts, but opened and fell as one connected part. A 56lb weight was attached to it by means of a cord. This cord passed through several small pulleys running along the lower portion of the platform, the idea being to prevent the trap from springing up again and hitting the body.

The platform was approximately 12' by 18' and rested on 6 strong supports. It was some 10' above the ground. On either side were uprights supporting a thick crossbeam. The rope, about 1¼" thick and with a running noose attached, hung from this beam.

Previous executions had been open to the public until quite recently; this one took place in private, in accordance with new regulations. Daly went to bed at 3am on the morning of his execution and slept until around 5.30. Wakened by warders, he got up, prayed and looked contrite. He attended mass at 6am and continued with his spiritual preparation until 8am when he was pinioned by the executioner (Marwood). Asked by the Sub-Sheriff (Bottomley) if he had any statement to make, Daly replied that he would like to thank the governor of the prison (Keough) and the other prison officials for their kind treatment of him.

Daly walked to the scaffold as if in a hurry. The expression on his face suggested that the very life had been squeezed out of him by fear. Once on the platform, the noose was put around his neck, his head covered with a hood, and the lever pulled.

Present at the execution were priests, the press, prison officials and several specially invited persons.

The prison bell ceased tolling and the black flag was run up. After an hour Daly's body was lowered, and placed in an ordinary deal coffin (painted black). The inquest was then conducted and Daly divested of his clothing, which became the property of the hangman. The coffin was filled with quicklime and the lid screwed down. Finally, Daly was buried within the prison grounds.

The Robert Street Murder
The Execution of Arthur McKeown
on 14th January 1889.

Arthur McKeown was executed at eight o'clock on the morning of
14.1.1889, within the precincts of the County Antrim Prison, (H.M.P.
Crumlin Road. Belfast).

Strenuous efforts were put forth by the condemned man's solicitor
and friends to secure a remission of the capital sentence, which
proved unavailing, and a like failure awaited the earnest appeal for
Vice-Regal clemency made in the name of a number of humane
gentlemen in Belfast. Memorials were submitted by Mr. Carr, founded
upon statements as to the existence of hereditary insanity in the
condemned man's family, which was a very natural and charitable
last resort, while the representations to Lord Londonderry from
influential citizens were doubtless based upon conscientious objection to the principle of capital punishment and a praiseworthy
desire to carry forward to the history of the then young city of Belfast
the exceptional record it possessed as a town with regard to the
execution of the dread penalty that stern justice exacts from the
shedder of human blood. For in the crime itself of extenuating
circumstances there were none.

The murder was a brutal and cold-blooded one sickening in its
details, for with more than bestial fury, batters and kicks a helpless
woman, returning again and again to his cowardly work until he has
not only crushed out the life, but obliterated the very semblance of
human shape and feature in the object of his barbarity, McKeown's
victim was his paramour, a fact which, far from mitigating his crime,
aggravated it, for the hapless creature, degraded though she might
have been, at least reposed confidence in him, and, as was shown,
bore even his brutal blows uncomplainingly. In short, there never
was a crime concerning which there was apparently less to pity and
more to condemn in its perpetrator, and never a crime in which the
royal prerogative of mercy, however strongly invoked, could have
been with so little warrant extended to stay the hand of justice. The
victim was Mary Jane Phillips, a woman about thirty years of age,
with whom McKeown cohabited at 38 Robert Street, off Academy
Street. The area was described during the period as one of the lowest
in Belfast. Phillips was found by the police in a dying condition in

the house in question. She was lying on the floor in a pool of blood, and bore marks of having been subjected to almost inconceivable barbarity. Her face, head, and body were literally covered with wounds, apparently caused by kicks or blows with some blunt instrument. The woman died almost immediately after the arrival of the police, and McKeown, whose hands and garments were saturated with blood, was arrested, and remanded pending the inquest. The medical evidence given before the coroner by Dr. S. Graham and McKee disclosed the fearful injuries which had caused the unfortunate woman's death, eight of her ribs were fractured, the aorta of the heart was ruptured, and several other terrible hurts, each almost mortal. The brutal and persistent violence which must have been exerted in order to produce these injuries may readily be imagined. At the magisterial inquiry which followed it was proved that McKeown had violently assaulted the deceased woman on the Saturday night in the house of a neighbour in Morrows Entry, and that she had afterwards been taken, or rather dragged, out of her house by him. Nothing more was seen of her or McKeown until the woman was found dying and McKeown in the house covered in her blood. Other evidence was forthcoming which left no doubt of his guilt, and he was committed for trial at the winter assizes, where on the 15th December last, before Mr. Justice Holmes, he was found guilty and sentenced to be hanged on the 14th January 1889.

McKeown had been married, but left his wife and went to live with the deceased a number of years previous. She had two children by him. McKeown's character was not good. He had formerly been a car driver, but for some time past had kept a small refreshment establishment at the house where the murder was committed. He was about thirty six years of age. Since his condemnation the culprit had behaved in an exemplary manner. From the first he seemed to have little or no hope that his sentence would be commuted. He maintained little interest in the efforts that he knew were being made on his behalf, and received the announcement of their failure with composure, even with indifference. According to the Rev. McAllister the Roman Catholic Chaplin, he ate slept and drank well. Though he left no statement of confession, it is understood that he acknowledged the justice of his sentence, and spoke with courage of his approaching fate. Once a week his sister and brother-in-law visited him, the last interview being on Saturday last, when, despite the distressing nature of the occasion, the culprit bore himself with firmness and courage, though he exhibited no want of natural feeling. Berry, the executioner, arrived on the Saturday morning, travelling from his home in Bradford by the London and North Western Railways and Fleetwood steamer. He was accompanied by his son, a boy of eight or ten, and an assistant from Blackpool. Although since his appointment to the gruesome office Berry had carried out upwards of a hundred executions in other parts of the United Kingdom. He was never required to do any executions in the north before this date. This was his first visit to Ulster, and his presence in Belfast attracted some little degree of morbid interest. He was accommodated in a house within the gaol grounds, near the Mater Hospital. Hangman Berry was a quiet looking individual, at about forty years of age, medium in height, and sandy hair. He was described as the principle actor in a hundred tragedies, he was more like a man engaged in contributing to varied coloured web of human life, than a kind of male clotho, whose business it was to sever the thread an uneducated man, doubtless, but withall possessing the native shrewdness of the Yorkshire man confined with the acquired assurance and confidence of the official man. From the very fact of him accepting such employment, should possess iron nerves and no superfluity of human feeling and who during the exercise of his occupation would probably have grown callous to the horror and repulsiveness of it. The reporter of the period stated, "early yesterday morning Berry and his assistant were engaged testing the scaffold, and making sure that the few details connected with the simple looking but cruel apparatus were in proper order". The young son of the executioner stood on the scaffold watching his father's movements. There was something repugnant in the idea of a child of tender years being familiarised with scenes as this. The structure of course was a temporary one, it was placed at the southern end of 'D' wing, and a door from the corridor of that wing opened directly on to the fatal platform. The latter was enclosed in on the other three sides with rough wooden boards, so as to screen the platform from possible observation from the windows of any of the neighbouring buildings. From a stout crossbeam above dangled the noose of death - a fearfully significant indication of the near approach of the last scene, and one which caused an involuntary shudder in the onlooker whom familiarity with such matters had not case-hardened. The rope, Berry fixed with great care, was a stout manila cord, three-eights of an inch in thickness. The noose was formed by what sailor called a cringle rove on one end of the rope, with an iron ring in the centre through which the opposite end was passed and carried to the beam above. In the middle of this platform was the drop or trap, an arrangement by which the portion of the flooring underneath the beam divided like a double trap door, opening downwards on hinges. When the bolt confined by the supporting bar was drawn, whatever was upon the trap launched into a pit below about eight feet deep. After testing the working parts carefully, Berry give it as his opinion that the drop was one of the best in England or Ireland. Outside the gaol, sometime before the ominous hour of eight, a crowd of several hundred persons gathered, mostly young fellows of the mill-hand class. They could see nothing but the dark outline of the gaol looming in the fog, but, with imagination many of them could map out clearly enough the picture of what was preparing and passing inside, they could even perhaps in their mind's eye see the one little group on the scaffold and the other in the chapel. Both groups preparing-for what? one to consign the body to shame and death, the other to send forward the soul on its mission with promise and hope. As the hour drew near the crowd grew denser and more dense, until a black mass extended from the corner of Agnes Street to the Mater Hospital. It is strange as to this morbid curiosity which has influenced men from the earliest times, which drew them with a kind of magnetic power to whatever a human being is to pass from lusty life to death under the awful authority of the law. Personality or respect of persons would appear to have little or no share in the origin of this feeling. The crowd waited in eagerness for the hoisting of the black flag on the gaol, which was the only outward and visible sign that told the nemesis had been satisfied within. By the permission of Mr.H.Bottomley, Sub-Sheriff of county Antrim, the members of the local press were permitted to witness the execution, the ordinary arrangements in connection with which were made by Mr. J.M'Kenna, deputy governor of the gaol, the death warrant, a solemn looking document with a deep border of black, was received by Mr. Bottomley from the Clerk of the Crown on Saturday and all hope of a respite departed yesterday evening. The Rev.J.McAllister, the chaplain, remained in the death cell until ten o'clock on Saturday night administering spiritual consolation to the condemned man, which the latter received with calmness and apparent penitence, although he seemed in other respects apathetic and almost indifferent to his approaching fate. He did not however, retire to rest until two o'clock on the morning of the hanging, and then slept calmly and peacefully until five, when being awakened by the warders, according to custom, he rose at once and dressed himself quietly, without betraying any signs of agitation, declining to take breakfast or any kind of refreshment. An hour later Father McAllister and his assistant entered the culprit's cell. The culprit proceeded to the chapel, where mass was celebrated, and where subsequently the holy communion was administered to him. At a few minutes before eight o' clock the melancholy procession from the chapel through the long corridor to the scaffold was formed, headed by the Sub-Sheriff, Dr. Stewart attended on each side by a warder, the deputy-governor and chief warder Coulter bring up the rear. McKeown was deadly pale, he walked with head bowed, his hands clasped upon a crucifix, which he held before him, but he moved firmly and without assistance. In a strong, unfaltering voice, but in an almost mechanical manner, he repeated the responses to the prayers for the dying. The convict was a small, slight built man, a countenance indicative of a low order of intellect, but one which would hardly give the idea of a man hardened in vice and brutalised by crime - a sharply receding forehead, a prominent nose, and deep set eyes. The footsteps of the living dead echoed on the march to the grave; the hollow tramp only broken by the solemn tolling of the chapel bell and the voice of the unfortunate appealing to heaven for the mercy which the earth had denied him. Cheeks involuntarily pale and lips tremble that would not blench at danger or quiver at moving scenes of ordinary woe. It was indeed an awful and solemn procession, a few yards from the door leading to the scaffold and executioner, who had been waiting near, steps forward with a board strap in his hand, with which he proceeds to pinion the arms of the culprit. It is the work of only a few moments. McKeown never lifts his eyes from the crucifix, to which his pinioned hands still cling. The executioner gives a sign, and again the sad group moves forward. The scaffold is reached, McKeown is handed over to the executioner who placed him on the trap beneath the beam, and with another strap binds his legs. The rope is quickly adjusted, the cringle or loop is placed just behind the left ear. The white cap is drawn over the face, the doomed man, standing firmly beneath the beam, exclaims loudly and fervently "Lord Jesus, receive my soul", "Lord, into thy hands I commend my spirit". Berry quickly steps aside, the fatal bolt is drawn by his assistants, the body disappears into the pit and a dozen seconds after he reaches the scaffold, Arthur McKeown had ceased to exist. Scarcely a motion of the rope could be detected. There was slight muscular movements of the face observable beneath the cap which covered the features, and that was all. McKeown was a man of 5 feet 8 inches in height, but very slight, being a little more than eight stone in weight. Berry give a drop of 7 feet which he stated would produce a force of more than a ton upon his neck. After allowing the body to remain hanging some minutes the executioner removed the cap from the face, and said sententiously, but not irreverently, quoting the words of Thistlewood, the Cato Street conspirator, "poor fellow, he knows the grand secret now". Immediately after the drop fell, the black flag was hoisted on the front of the prison, and the chapel bell continued to toll for some time.

The inquest was quite a long and tedious affair, but I have condensed it and made appropriate observations as to its contents. At noon the jurors assembled at the prison, and were soon afterwards admitted, as the inquiry was fixed for a quarter past twelve. On entering the gaol they were conducted to the board room, where they remained for a brief period. Mr.H.Bottomley, Mr.H.Neile M'Cormick, Clerk of the Crown for County Antrim, District Inspector M'Ardle, and Mr.Jermiah M'Kenna, Deputy Governor of the prison, were in attendance. When Dr.Dill, Borough Coroner, arrived, he at once asked that the jury should be taken to the place where the remains of the deceased lay, in order that they might inspect them. They were then taken along the corridor, down which in the morning the procession went when McKeown was being conducted to the scaffold. Within a few feet from the corridor was a coffin containing the body of the culprit. The coffin, which rested on two stools, was of plain deal, coloured black, and was quite an improvement on the very primitively constructed rough box in which the remains of Daly were shown to the jurors after his execution some twelve years earlier. A couple of warders stood by, as the coroner and jurors approached, one of them removed the coffin lid, and there lay before them the body of the deceased. The sight was not by any means a pleasant one. The left eye, which was much swollen, was to use a familiar expression, quite "black" while the features bore the reverse of a peaceful aspect. From the place where the coffin was, a good view could be obtained through the large end window of the corridor of the exterior of one side of the scaffold, which stood close by. It was while the jurors were standing round the coffin that they were sworn in by Dr. Dill. They were as follows: Messrs. Thomas Conroy, C.B. Officer, 13 Ponsonby Avenue; Robert Dick, Pensioner, Woodland Avenue; Robert Wilson, T.C.Contractor, 8 Cavendish Terrace, Henry Scott, Druggist, Eia Street; Patrick Quigley, Spirit Merchant, 18 Hillman Street; Patrick Leonard, Hotel keeper, Duncairn Arms; John Corkerin, R.I.C.Pensioner; John M'Auley, Lamplighter, 4 Ashton Street; William J.Rankin, Druggist, 173 New Lodge Road; John Wilson, Ex-Head Constable R.I.C. Stratheden Street; William J.Campell, R.I.C. Pensioner, 11 Cranburn Street, George Wilson, Publican, Carlisle, Circus; Robert Beattle, Publican, Denmark Street; William Shields, Publican, Denmark Street, John Trainor, Publican, Old Lodge Road; Clements Bell, Flesher, Old Lodge Road; David Ferguson, Publican, Old Lodge Road; John Andrews, Grocer, Old Lodge Road, William H.Campbell, boot and shoe maker, 46 Arkwright Street; William Kelly, Grocer, 119 Old Lodge Road.

There were twenty persons on the jury compared to twelve on the trail jury. They then returned to the board room, when several of them said they would like to see the scaffold. Dr. Dill conveyed this request to Mr.M'Kenna, Deputy Governor, who took them to the structure, which they examined very closely. They were accompanied by Sergeant Carnaghan, who had summoned the jury and had charge of the arrangement connected with inquest. On returning to the board room evidence was received:-

Date of the murder - 26th August 1888.

How long was the prisoner remended? - Untill the 1st September, and on that day he was committed for trial on the charge of murder, and he remained in the governors custody until the day of execution.

Dr. Dill asked Mr. H.H.Bottonly who was the Sub-Sheriff for the county of Antrim, did he witness the execution by Berry?

Mr Bottonly -Yes. I saw him pinion and hang him.

(Then there was an odd question) What is Berry's Christian names? Witness - I do not know.

A Juror - Is there any chance of the jury having any means of seeing the implement or rope by which this man came to his death?

Dr.Dill (to witness) - Is the rope in your possession?

Witness - No it belongs to Berry himself, he took it with him.

Mr. Robert Wilson - There are a great many here who are anxious that Berry should be produced.

Dr. Dill (to witness) - Have you any knowledge where he is?

Witness - I have no idea. I have no power over him. A request might effect that purpose? I have not the slightest idea where he is. I was only to glad to get him away - even out by the back way.

Mr. Wilson, (to witness) - What size or height was he?

Witness - Well, now, he was just about the size and height of that man sitting beside you, and he had a red beard.

Mr. Bottomley was called and he stated that the body was handed over to him and he handed it over to James Berry, the public executioner, who carried out the sentence in his presence, and that sentence was that he be hanged by the neck until he was dead.

A Juror - I suppose you don't know where Mr.Berry is either?

Witness - No, I do not.

Mr.R.Wilson - When was the last time you saw him?

Witness - I saw him about a quarter past nine o'clock. He asked me if he might go, and I said yes.

A Juror - Do the implements he uses belong to him?

Witness - He himself provided the rope and pinioning straps.

A Juror - Is it a rope or chain he uses for going round the neck?

Witness - It is a rope I saw it.

Another Juror - Do you not consider Mr. Bottomley that it would be more satisfactorily for a jury and the public at large if they could see the appliance whereby this man came to his death?

Witness - I do not.

The same juror - In the carrying out of the law I think it would be more satisfactory if the jury and the public at large, that at a public execution (Witness - This was not a public execution.)

The juror - In the carrying out of a sentences it would be more satisfactory if the jury heard from the lips of the man who takes away the life of his fellow man and the manner whereby he took away that life.

Witness - I cannot agree with you.

The juror - I think it would be more in keeping with the circumstances if that person was retained to give evidence that he had carried out the law. He alone can give that evidence.

Witness - The Coroner can give his expression of opinion as to whether or not sufficient evidence had been adduced.

Dr. Dill - We will get the medical evidence, and medical testimony in this as indeed in almost every other court is the accepted authority as to the cause of death. One of the gentlemen we have heard, or even the public executioner himself, is an authority upon the subject of death, but the doctor can tell us too and will give evidence now. While every gentlemen upon the jury is perfectly right in expressing his opinion on this and any other subjects, yet I may say that in the law the only authority upon the cause of death, or death itself, is the medical witness.

Witness - I may mention that Berry, who, as you know carried out a great number of executions in England says he was never required or asked before a jury yet.

Dr. Dill - The jury will agree with me when I say that while there may be no absolute statute or law on the subject, yet precedent and custom, and, I think I am speaking in the presence of gentlemen who know the law, often comes in its stead. I think there is no precedent or custom by which the public executioner had ever to attend the enquiry.

A juror - I don't think it would be a bad job to introduce it. It is not yet too late.

Dr. Dill - That is another matter.

A juror - I as one juror, protest against the custom of the executioner being smuggled out of the back door of the prison.

Mr.Bottomley - I do not think that that expression is warranted.

Dr. Dill - These executions in gaols are carried out in private, and I think very properly, for public's decency's sake. But afterwards there is an inquest held to see that the matter is carried out according to law. Seeing that that is the case, I left word at the gate that any person who had an interest in this inquiry should not be shut out. This jury is a public inquiry, although the execution is absolutely and by law private.

Mr.R.Wilson - Seeing that this is a public inquiry, we should have all persons connected with the execution present, and hangman Berry has been asked for by some of the juror's.

Dr.Dill - I am a physician, surgeon, and medical officer of Her Majesty's Prison Belfast. I was present this morning, at eight o'clock. By hanging there was no struggle or muscular movements except three small tremors of the face as seen by the movements of the whitecap, which occurred at intervals for a period of two and a quarter minutes after the drop. On examination of the body after it was taken down at 9am. I found the head leaning on the right shoulder the rotatory movements being more than natural. In my opinion death was almost instantaneous, and was caused by injury to the spinal cord at the seat of dislocation.

Dr. Dill - This occurrence to the neck took place by hanging?

Witness - Yes.

A juror - There are a number of the jury who are anxious for an explanation of the cause of the black eye. There appeared to be a lump.

Witness - The flesh is swollen, the rope came round the right side of the neck, and came up at the left, and the blood in the large veins would be more or less stopped, which would produce the contusion of that part.

Juror - You believe that was the cause?

Witness - Yes.

Dr. Dill - You don't know what state of health he was in previously?

Witness - He was in good health last night at ten o'clock.

Dr. Dill - What was his health since his committal?

Witness - Good.

Dr. Dill - How did he eat and drink?

Witness - He ate and drank and slept fairly well.

Dr. Dill - Did he eat his breakfast that morning?

Witness - I did not ascertain.

Dr. Dill - Did he get any refreshments this morning and what were his refreshments to have been?

Witness - His breakfast would have been bacon and eggs, tea and toast.

Dr. Dill - You don't know whether or not he partook of it?

Witness - I do not. The deputy governor can tell.

Mr. Mc Kenna - No sir. He was in at communion this morning. He did not partake of it at all. His Chaplin was with him from about half past six o'clock.

Dr. Dill - And he was so occupied with his Chaplin that he took no breakfast?

Witness - Yes.

Dr. Dill - And the Chaplin was present at the execution?

Witness - Yes.

A juror - There are a number of jurors who are desirous of seeing the room which the deceased had occupied since his committal, and if there were any changes made when he was under the sentence of death?

Witness - I believe, according to law, there is considerable relaxation with regard to prisoners under sentence of death, and that might be inquired into from the deputy governor.

Mr. Mc Kenna - He was in what we would call a double room, two single cells. They were very comfortable indeed, in fact they had been occupied by one of the officers before. There was a fireplace and a fire and every other comfort.

Dr. Dill - Do you give the prisoners fires?

Mr. Mc Kenna - The cells are heated by hot water, but, there being a fireplace in the room a fire was kept in it. Anything he wanted he got, and was told that that would be the case.

Dr. Dill - Did he get any stimulants?

Witness - He did?

Dr. Dill - What were the stimulants?

Dr. Stewart - Immediately after his sentence he was greatly depressed. He got an ounce of brandy every three hours for thirty hours. Then he got two bottles of stout and three ounces of whiskey every twenty four hours up till the refusal of a reprieve. From that day he got three bottles of stout and five ounces of whiskey every twenty four hours. He got tea and toast for supper, and mutton chop and beef steak alternately with vegetables and potatoes for dinner. He got half an ounce of tobacco daily.

Dr Dill (to Mr. Mc Kenna) - Would you have any objection to allowing the jury to see the room?

Mr. Mc Kenna - It is against the rule. but three or four of them may come.

Dr. Stewart - The room is, I believe, 14ft by 7ft.

Mr. Wilson - Is the room kept for murderers or gentlemen prisoners?

Mr. Mc Kenna - It is a room I would sleep in myself. It is a very comfortable room and was once used by one of the officials. I will show it to you if you like. McKeown had expressed entire satisfaction at the way he had been treated. He frequently expressed his satisfaction at his treatment by all the officials.

A juror (to the Governor) - Did he give any expression as to whether he was undergoing the sentence of the law justly?

Witness - I cannot state.

A Juror - Did he make a public confession?

Witness - No.

A Juror - Has he left any statement in writing?

Mr. Mc Kenna - No he has not. Although I believe he was perfectly reconciled, and, if anything, more anxious to die than live.

The jury then returned the following verdict:-

That the said Arthur McKeown on the 14th day of January, 1889, in due form of law, and in pursuance and execution of a judgment of death passed upon him at the assizes, held at Belfast aforesaid, in and for same county, on Thursday, 6th day of December 1888, for the murder of Mary Philips, was hanged by the neck until he was dead at the common place of execution within the walls of the prison aforesaid, being the prison in which he was confined at the time of his execution.

This terminated the proceedings. Some of them went to see the cell in which McKeown had been confined from the time he was sentenced to death. During the inquest the Coroner gave permission to the prison officials to inter the remains and this, we believe, was done immediately afterwards.

The Dervock Murder
The Execution of John Gilmore on 17th August 1894

JohnGilmore was hanged in Belfast Prison for the murder of an elderly farmer, Lyle Gardner, at Ballyhavistock, near Dervock, on 30th April 1894.

Gilmore was the son of respectable Presbyterian parents from Ballyhavistock. He committed the murder which would cost him his own life at the age of twenty-one. Gardner, his victim, who lived not far from the Gilmore's, was seventy eight and had been married twice. He had a daughter, considerably older than Gilmore, by his first marriage, and a son by his second.

Jane, his daughter, and Gilmore had been 'acquainted' with one another for some time. When she gave birth to a child, she alleged that Gilmore had fathered it. The rumours soon reached Gilmore, as did the news that the unborn child's grandfather was threatening to begin legal proceedings against him. So, on Monday 30th April 1894, he travelled from Ballyhavistock to Dervock, had a horse shod, and hired a car. which he drove to Ballymoney. He partook of some whiskey en route, and, arriving in Ballymoney, purchased a gun, powder and shot, a razor and several items of jewellery, and drove back home.

Before he reached Dervock, however, he got out of the car and told the driver to take a long parcel (containing the gun) to a hostelry where, he said, he would collect it later. The driver did as he was asked. Gilmore, after collecting his father's horse from the blacksmith's forge where he had left it, called for his parcel.

Later that evening, at around eight o'clock, the Gardners and a servant named Rogers were sitting in their kitchen when Mrs. Gardner saw a face at the window. Rogers went out into the yard and found Gilmore. The Gardners followed out. Gilmore wanted to know if they were blaming him for their daughter's pregnancy and if they intended to take him to court in Ballymena. There were no ugly scenes and the Gardners went inside again.

Shortly afterwards, as Mr. Gardner was undressing by the fireside, a shot was fired through the window which hit him. He died a few hours later.

When the R.I.C. got wind of this incident they set about making inquiries. They then made their way to Gilmore's house. They found him lying awake in the bedroom he shared with a younger brother, who was asleep. He was ordered to get up and come quietly. On the way downstairs something fell to the ground, and, at Gilmore's feet the police found a canister of powder. He was promptly arrested and charged with the murder of Mr. Gardner. In reply he gave an alibi and stated that he had been at the Wilson's all evening. The following day the R.I.C. discovered a gun, later identified as similar to that bought by Gilmore in Ballymoney, under a bush between the Gardner and Gilmore homes. On Tuesday May 1st an inquest on the body was opened but was adjourned for two days as the coroner was taken ill.

The investigation proper was presided over by Mr. William Orr, R.M., in the Dervock Courthouse on Tuesday May 8th. The Crown was represented by Mr. J. Carr and the accused by Mr. R. Martin and Mr. Taggart of Ballymoney. The evidence was looked into and it emerged that Gilmore had lied when he had told the sergeant, who had picked up the flask of gunpowder, that he had bought it at Rea's in Dervock. The objects found on the person of the accused when arrested were identified as similar to those sold on the day of the murder. Jane Gardner was called as a witness and after giving her evidence she swore that Gilmore was the father of her child.

The result of all this was that Gilmore was returned for trial on the capital charge. On Wednesday 18th July, he was arraigned thereupon in the County Courthouse before Mr. Justice Gibson and an Antrim jury.

The prisoner pleaded not guilty, and was defended by Mr. O'Shaughnessy and Mr. George Hill Smith. After a hearing which continued for a few days, the jury found Gilmore guilty of murder but recommended strongly that he be shown mercy on the grounds of his youth and previous good character.

The sentence of death was, however, pronounced in the time honoured way and the execution pencilled in for the 17th of August. Gimore persisted with his declarations of innocence in a careful and determined, if not skilful, murder.

His solicitor and friends worked tirelessly on his behalf in their efforts to have the death sentence commuted but their efforts were in vain. The authorities insisted that the law must run its course and Gilmore received the news of the failure of the petitions on his behalf with resignation. Since sentenced he had eaten well, increased slightly in height, but slept very badly. He was visited regularly by

47

the Rev. Dr. Crawford, Presbyterian Chaplain, and the Rev. Joseph Northey, who, during the former absences, stood in for him. Gilmore paid the utmost attention to their ministrations and although betraying some signs of emotion for the first time since his confinement, could not have been described as downcast. His mother and father also visited him and their interviews with their son were of the most affecting nature.

On his final Monday morning Gilmore at last confessed his guilt and expressed deepest sorrow for his crime. He had, he said, never intended to kill old Gardner until the morning of the crime. He felt his punishment was just and well deserved. The execution took place at eight o'clock and, unlike previous hangings in the Crumlin Road, was strictly private. Only prison officials were present with the press being excluded.

Gilmore's cell was on the left hand side of the corridor running the full length of D.Wing. This corridor extends eastwards towards Carlisle Circus. The scaffold was erected at the very end of it in an enclosure adjoining the boundary wall of the prison. It was situated about thirty feet from the cell and the platform was on a level with the corridor, so that the condemned man could neither see whether he was going nor realise exactly when the drop would occur.

On the night before his execution Gilmore slept fairly well. The following morning he breakfasted lightly on tea and toast. He showed no signs of nervousness or excitement, but appeared resigned to an ignominious death in a few hours thence.

The following official account of the execution was supplied to the press:

At 6am the chaplains of the prison, Rev Dr. Crawford, and the Rev. J. Northey entered the prison and conducted divine service in the condemned man's cell. They were still engaged when the Sub-Sheriff arrived shortly before half past seven.

A few minutes before eight o'clock, accompanied by the governor, the Sub-Sheriff proceeded to the cell, where, according to usage, the latter demanded from Mr. Murphy the body of John Gilmore.

The governor thereupon gave Gilmore into the custody of the Sheriff, and Mr. Bottomley asked the prisoner if he had any statement or observation to make. Gilmore immediately replied in a steady voice:-

I admit the justice of the sentence passed upon me. I am very sorry for the crime I have committed and for my sins and I hope to obtain

48

mercy from God.

The Sub-Sheriff then asked Gilmore if he had anything to say about the treatment he had received in prison and in reply Gilmore expressed his warmest thanks for the kindness shown to him by the governor and other officials.

Gilmore then shook hands with the governor and the wardens of his own religious persuasion who had attended him throughout his stay in prison. He also shook hands with the chaplains who had been assiduous in their attentions to him, thanking both in the heartiest manner.

A procession then formed up. At the head was the Chaplin, reciting the burial service for the dead. Then came the prisoner, wearing his own clothes, but barefaced. On each side of him was a warder, with one behind. In the rear were the Sub-Sheriff, the governor, and prison doctor.

It was but a short distance from the condemned cell to the scaffold. The procession had gone only a few steps when the executioner, Scott, stepped out from an adjoining cell unperceived, and, coming up behind Gilmore, pinioned his arms with short straps. After this short interruption the procession moved off again. The Rev. Dr. Crawford repeated prayers and Gilmore responded to them in an audible voice all the way. Gilmore was showing a considerable amount of emotion by this stage, yet he walked steadily to the scaffold, repeating time and time again: 'The Lord have mercy upon my soul.' He kissed the warders, and, just as he was positioned over the trapdoor, turned slightly and said; 'Farewell to all my friends till we all meet again.'

As Gilmore was saying this, Scott was pinioning his legs, and, just as he was finishing speaking, the executioner slipped a white linen cap over his head. The bolt was withdrawn immediately, the trap fell, Gilmore disappeared from view, and the rope twitched.

Death, according to Dr Stewart, was almost instantaneous. Gilmore weighed 9st 8lbs and was allowed a drop of six feet. Chaplin Crawford, in conversation with the Sub-Sheriff, said that it was his first experience of such a trying ordeal. He had attended many deathbeds but could remember no - one more penitent than Gilmore. The scene outside the prison was unusual. The crowd, which numbered several thousands and consisted mostly of mill - workers on their way to work, began to gather at 6.30 am. The police were also represented but were not called upon as the crowd was respectful and sympathetic throughout its vigil.

At precisely 8 am the black flag was hoisted on the roof of the main building: it was all over. The prison-bell tolled for about ten minutes after the execution. A jury was empanelled in readiness for the inquest.

At 10am the City Coroner, Mr E. Finnigan, and the members of the jury arrived at the prison and were shown into the boardroom, where the inquest on Gilmore's remains was held. The proceedings were a mere formality. Immediately after being sworn in, the jury, along with the coroner, inspected the body of the deceased. Gilmore's corpse had been cut down after hanging for an hour and placed in a cell. They later inspected the scaffold as well.

Gilmore's face, only slightly discoloured, looked tranquil and exhibited no sign of suffering. The mark left by the rope was barely perceptible.

The Coroner then addressed the jury. As they were aware, executions had formerly taken place in public. However, owing to the terrible scenes witnessed at such events, legislation had been enacted to provide for executions to be carried out within the precincts of prisons. Guidelines had been laid down as to who should attend, and inspection of the deceased by a jury was provided for. Such juries were also to examine evidence to ensure that the law had been properly adhered to.

Finnigan was sure that many of the jurors would have wished that the legislature had gone one step further and abolished capital punishment altogether. He thought it would have been desirable if the taking of life had been left to the giver of it.

The following verdict was drawn up by the Coroner, and returned and signed by the jury:

...that the said John Gilmore, being a male person of the age of twenty-two years, and a farmer, was a prisoner in the County Antrim Prison, under judgment of death was duly executed on him by being hanged by the neck until dead, within the walls of the said prison, on the 17th day of August 1894, not more than twenty-four hours before the holding of this inquest...

The foreman stated that the jury wished to express its sincere sympathy for the parents of both the unfortunate murderer, whose life had been taken away that morning, and for the widow of the murdered man. He requested the Coroner to convey this message.

Mr Finnigan concurred with the suggestion, saying that he would ensure that the jury's message would be forwarded at once. The proceedings then terminated.

The Bushmills Murder
The Execution of William Woods
on 1st November 1901

William Woods was executed on the morning of 1st November 1901 at Belfast Prison. His hanging was the culmination of a series of events which shocked the north Antrim community like none before. Woods, aged fifty-eight, a pedlar, had murdered Bridget McGivern, a widow from Bushmills, a town more famous for its whiskey than for events such as the one to be recounted here.

McGivern and her two children tenanted an impoverished cabin near the town. On 25th September, Woods, an old acquaintance dropped by. He brought a bottle of the old whiskey, and the two of them, Woods and McGivern, sat drinking into the wee small hours. Little did McGivern know what was in store for her. Woods did; it was later established that the murder was premeditated. Woods asked if he could stay the night, sleeping in the kitchen. Next morning, as McGivern went about setting a fire in that room, Woods pounced on her, and, with a razor he had bought the day before, came close to severing her head from her body. He then made his way to the local R.I.C. station and, covered in blood, turned himself in. There was no motive for the crime. Woods had murdered McGivern most brutally and constant drinking, it seemed, lay behind it all.

During the trial, and even later, when already sentenced to death, Woods relentlessly and callously made light of his situation, making merry of the murder, saying it was 'little worse than a bad marriage.' To the administrations of the chaplain, the Rev Dr Spence of St Mary's Parish, however, Woods paid deep and sincere heed. Indeed, as the morning of the execution neared, the condemned man's entire demeanour changed. Whereas before he had been heedless and callous, he was now penitent, humiliated and prayerful. Despite this though, he remained outwardly firm until the Sunday, when he broke down while attending divine service in the prison chapel.

Throughout his period of incarceration Woods was treated with kindness not only by the chaplain and prison medical officer, Dr Stewart, but also by the officials.

Accorded the traditional privileges of men sentenced to death,

Woods was allowed, as far as diet was concerned, pretty well whatever he wanted. He limited himself, though, to tea, toast, eggs and beef-tea. On top of this he was allowed two glasses of whiskey every day. His health improved and his weight increased by 20lbs. On the Thursday, Woods grew very restless and touched little food, declining all stimulants. He could not sleep that night and, on the Friday morning, was unable to eat at first. Obviously weak and nervous, he was prevailed upon by the prison doctor to at least take some food extracts.

From 7am a considerable crowd had been gathering outside the prison, watching for the hoisting of the black flag which indicated that a 'life for a life' had been taken.

Inside the gloomy prison a very sad scene indeed was taking place. As the clock struck a quarter to eight, the Chaplain administered the last rites of the Episcopal Church to Woods. The Sub-Sheriff of County Antrim (Bottomley) then arrived with Dr Stewart and, entering the condemned man's cell, presented the death warrant to the prison governor (McManus). As this happened the chapel bell began to toll.

Outside, the crowd fell silent.

At ten minutes to eight, the executioner (Scott) and his assistant, pinioned Woods, who seemed suddenly to realise that he had but a few minutes to live. He wept and prayed loudly as they proceeded the short distance towards the scaffold. He had to be supported by a warder. The procession moved along slowly, passing through a doorway into a small room on the same floor.

The scaffold had been erected only recently. Below it was a 'well' into which the body dropped after the trap-door opened.

A few minutes before eight Scott pinioned Woods' legs and the chaplain recited the burial service. Just before the white cap was drawn over his face, the haggard Woods cast a pathetic look around the room, closed his eyes and prayed. Then, as he stood on the trap, the rope was adjusted around his neck. On the stroke of eight, Scott pushed the lever, the bolt was withdrawn, the trap fell, and Woods vanished.

The crowd saw the black flag appear, muttered expressions of pity, and went about their daily business.

Within three hours the inquest was held, chaired by the City Coroner (Finnigan). The public were represented by a jury and the police by Head-Constable Sargeant and Sergeant Murphy. Reporters also viewed the body which had been laid out in the execution chamber. There was no outward sign that Woods had been hanged; his neck was almost unmarked, and the prison doctor described the execution as one of the most successful he had ever known.

The inquest passed off without incident. The Chaplain noted that Woods had not complained during his incarceration and had admitted his guilt. Dr Stewart noted that Woods, although somewhat debilitated on admission to the prison, suffering from the effects of drinking, he had been in good health generally. The doctor, in reply to the Coroner's questions, did not consider a post-mortem necessary; he had already made a superficial examination. Death had been caused by dislocation of the neck and was instantaneous. The Coroner noted that in England it was customary to hold a post-mortem after an execution, but, in this case, it was unnecessary, unless the jury objected. The jury did not object and returned a verdict in accordance with the medical evidence.

The Execution of Richard Justin
on 19th August 1909

'Justice For Justin', screamed the newspaper headlines after Richard Justin, a labourer, was condemned to death at the City Assizes in Belfast for the murder of his four-year-old child in Lepper Street in March 1909.

Justin had been in the habit of systematically and brutally beating the child until, finally, his cruelty culminated in the infliction of injuries so severe that they resulted in death, the infant succumbing to a cerebral haemorrhage caused by blows to the head.

The doctor who examined the child's body found it to be covered in bruises, and it was proved in evidence that Justin had beaten the child with an iron rod. For the defence it was alleged that the injuries had been caused by the child falling out of bed.

After sentence of death had been passed, a petition praying for a reprieve was sent by Justin's friends to the Lord Lieutenant, but His Excellency saw no reason for interfering with the course of law. Justin however, seemed to cherish the hope that his life would be spared; when the decision of the Viceroy was communicated to him, he at first seemed to give way to despair, but, as his final hours approached, he became calmer, listening to the exhortations of the Unitarian minister, Rev F. Wooley of the Stanhope Mission, who attended to him devotedly until the very end.

Justin had a farewell interview with his reatives on the Wednsday before his execution.

He arose early on the morning of August 19th after a restless night and accepted with apparent devoutness and resignation the consolations of Mr Wooley. He then breakfasted. Shortly before 8am the Governor of the prison (Mr Stringer), the City High Sheriff (Councillor Francis Curly J.P.), the Sub-Sheriff (Mr James Quail), and the executioner (Pierpont, who had arrived the night before and slept within the precincts of the prison) entered the cell.

As the chapel bell tolled, the melancholy procession made its way from the condemned cell to the execution chamber, a permanent structure built in 1900. It was only a few paces from the cell and on the same floor. Justin walked without assistance, although a Chief Warder and an Assistant Warder were in attendance to support the prisoner if necessary. Also present were the prison's Chief Medical

Officer (Dr John Stewart) and the Reverend Wooley.

Apart from these officials, no-one was permitted to witness the execution - a very proper and salutary development on the part of the authorities. From the evidence offered at the inquest, however, and from the statements made by those who were present, it would appear that the sentence was carried out with merciful dispatch. The condemned man's arms were pinioned in the corridor by the executioner and, as the procession went, Mr Wooley recited prayers. Justin did not speak, but moved mechanically and seemed dazed. At the scaffold Pierpont strapped the prisoner's legs together, put the white hood over his head and, on the stroke of eight, pulled the lever which released the trap-door. Death seemed to be instantaneous; the wretched man's neck was dislocated by the fall.

After hanging for the prescribed time, the body was taken down and placed in a coffin, pending the inquest, which was held at 10am. After this, the remains were interred within the prison walls.

Although there was absolutely no chance of seeing the execution from outside the jail and even the practice of hoisting the black flag to signal the execution of a prisoner had been dispensed with, the crowds, driven by a morbid curiosity, had assembled as the hour of Justin's execution neared. They represented, almost to a man, the dregs of society: the unemployed and the unemployable.

While some seemed satisfied with hearing the tolling of the chapel bell, most hung around until the official notices, signed by the authorities (the High Sheriff, the Sub-Sheriff, the Governor, the Doctor and clergyman), were posted on the prison gates. This notice stated that the execution had been duly carried out and, as they were posted, there was a surge towards the gates and policemen had to repel the crowd.

It had been some eight years since the last execution in Belfast. There had been several death sentences passed in the County Courthouse, but these were on men from other Ulster counties, sent for trial, and returned for execution. William Woods, a tramp, was the last man hanged in Belfast; his crime was the murder of a peasant woman named McGivern near Bushmills in County Antrim. Woods incidentally, had already murdered once before, in a particularly brutal manner, but had only been brought to justice after his second killing. At 10am the City Coroner, Dr James Graham, visited the prison to hold the inquest into Justin's death. The jury, whose foreman was Mr William Tougher JP, viewed the body and proceeded to the

56

Governor's office, where the inquiry was conducted. The police were represented by Head-Constable Moore.

Mr Quail, Sub-Sheriff, said that he had been present at the Summer Assizes on 22nd July when Justin stood trial, was convicted of the murder of his daughter, Annie Thompson, and sentenced to death. Acting on behalf of the High Sheriff, he had subsequently received from the Clerk of the Crown and Peace, the warrant for the execution, which he now produced. He had attended the execution that morning, carried out in accordance with the law and in pursuance of the death warrant.

Mr Stringer, the Governor, said that the deceased had been brought to the prison on 19th March 1909 on a charge of wilful murder. He had subsequently been tried and convicted at the last Summer Assizes upon that charge and sentenced to death. The execution had taken place that morning in accordance with the rules and in the presence of himself and other officials.

Dr John Stewart of 10 Carlisle Terrace said he was the Medical Officer at Belfast Jail. The witness had examined the deceased on 19th March and seen him frequently thereafter; he had been present at the execution that morning. There had been no abrasions, except for a slight mark or discolouration caused by the rope used. In the witness's opinion death had been due to dislocation of the vertebrae of the neck by hanging. The execution had been carried out quickly and expeditiously; death had been instantaneous.

Asked by the Coroner if he had anything to say, the High Sheriff (Mr Francis Curly, JP) said that ever since he had first come into contact with Justin and the Governor and officials at the prison, he had been deeply gratified by the kindness and attention the latter had shown the deceased. He could hardly believe, and was touched by, the sympathy Justin had been shown. Even Justin's relatives could hardly have been as sympathetic. The prisoner had thanked them for this sympathy and expressed very sincere regret.

That morning Justin had sent his prayers and good wishes to his mother, father and children (to whom he also sent some religious books which friends had kindly brought him). The execution itself had barely taken a moment; the witness, Curly, could not have imagined that such a thing was possible. Justin had walked to the scaffold.

The Coroner said that he was sure that the jury would agree with him when he said that they had heard a very satisfactory statement from the High Sheriff. He could only endorse what had already been said. He had always found that Mr Stringer discharged his duties sympathetically.

The jury was satisfied that the execution had been carried out satisfactorily, and that death had taken place naturally; it returned a verdict in accordance with the medical evidence.

The Cavehill Murder
The Execution of Simon McGeown
on 17th August 1922

Simon Mc Geown was hanged in Belfast Jail at 8am on Thursday 30th May 1922 for the murder of seven year old Maggie Fullerton on Cavehill.

A sizable crowd gathered outside the prison on Crumlin Road. The prison bell did not toll, and no black flag was hoisted. The only intimation that McGeown had been executed was the posting of the customary notice on the prison gates. It was signed by the prison`s Deputy Governor (Thomas Moore Stuart), the Rev Joseph Northey, the Sub - Sheriff (Mr James Quail.) The executioner was Ellis, assisted by Willis.

McGeown had slept well the previous evening and had risen at 6.30am. He had breakfasted heartily. He seemed stoical to the end. The scaffold had been erected and all the preliminaries dealt with the previous day. McGeown walked firmly to it after being pinioned by the hangman.

Afterwards the City Coroner, Dr. James Graham, held an inquest into McGeown's death. All the usual formalities were dealt with; everything had been done by the book, in accordance with the law and the arrangements made for the carrying out of the death penalty. Death had been instantaneous, according to Dr. P. O' Flaherty. The left side of the neck was slightly discoloured, the cervical vertebrae dislocated.

Little Maggie Fullerton had not enjoyed such a swift death. She had been lured away from her playmates off Little York Street on the evening of May 30th 1922. Her mutilated body had been found in a plantation on the Belfast Castle Demense by Lord Shaftesbury's gamekeeper. Mc Keown had been arrested and tried before Lord Justice Andrews.

The prosecution (Mr. John Mc Gonigal) described the murder as most horrible and brutal. The body had not been discovered for four days; it had been buried below leaves and rubbish on the Shaftesbury estate. The child had been interfered with and then murdered. Mc Geown had been seen taking the child away from the street, and a farmer on Cavehill testified that he had seen the accused man carrying the child through fields. Dr. N. Graham's medical evidence revealed shocking injuries. Death had been caused by a fracture of the skull.

No evidence was called for the defence. Mr. G. Hanna, addressing the members of the jury on behalf of the accused, said that the crime was of an appalling nature, and that the jury should therefore be all the more careful in reaching a decision.

The judge, in his charge to the jury, said that the case was one of the most awful he had ever had the misfortune to come across in a court of law. The jury, after deliberating for three quarters of an hour, returned a verdict of guilty. Representations were made to the Minister for Home Affairs in regard to a reprieve but were unsuccessful.

McGeown had seen long military service in India, suffering from sunstroke and malaria. During the Great War he was thrice wounded and twice gassed.

The Execution of Michael John Pratley
on 8th May 1924

Pratley was found guilty of the murder of Nelson Leach (on 7th March 1924) and sentenced to death of 10th April of the same year. The judge described the murder of Mr. Leach, an employee of Purdy & Millard Sculptors, as a cowardly crime. Pratley and two accomplices were evidently acquainted with the office procedures at Purdy & Millard. On the afternoon of the murder, Mr. Leach had withdrawn a large sum of cash, the firm's wages, from the Anne St. Branch of the Ulster Bank. He then returned to the offices, shortly before 3 pm. He and a clerk were about to make up the pay when three armed masked men forced their way into the room. There is some confusion as to what exactly happened next. This much is certain: Leach and the clerk were told to put their hands up; a shot was fired; there was a brief struggle; another shot was fired; Leach was hit and fell to the ground. The robbers panicked and fled. One of them disappeared up Hamill St, the other two made off up Galway St. The latter were chased by a lady employee of Purdy & Millard. The RUC had by now been alerted, and an officer (Constable Morteshed), seeing the lady, caught up with her. She informed him of what had happened. He turned into Barrack St, where he saw Pratley acting suspiciously. The officer placed him under arrest. Pratley, who had discarded his mask by this stage, produced a handgun, pressed it against the officer's side and pulled the trigger. The officer was more fortunate than Leach; the gun misfired. Pratley was then disarmed and hauled off to the nearby police station. Pratley's gun, a revolver, contained eight cartridges; one of them had been discharged but not ejected. It was later proven that the bullet which had caused Leach's death (Leach died in Belfast's Royal Victoria shortly after the bungled hold-up) was similar in type to those left in the revolver and to others found on Prately's person. The other bullet fired by the robbers was found embedded in the door of the telephone box in the office; it was a different calibre, which suggested that another robber had fired it. Pratley, a tailor by trade, was a married man with children from Moira St, Belfast. His trail caused a great deal of public interest; the public, of course, was outraged by the incident at the sculptors'. The accused man maintained an air of indifference throughout the preliminary investigations and later at the City Commission. The trial took a sensational turn when the defence counsel called Pratley to the witness-box. The defendant admitted openly that he had taken part in the hold-up, the object of which had been to steal the firm's wages. With equal openness, Prately admitted that he had fired a shot, but claimed to have aimed above Leach. The Attorney-General tried to extract from Prately a statement as to who had fired the fatal shot, but all Prately was prepared to say - and he said it with firm resolution - was: 'I am not prepared to answer that.' When it was put to him that he was 'sheltering his chum', he merely smiled and steadfastly declined to implicate anyone else in the crime. Then came another sensation; the Attorney-General handed Prately a letter, and asked him if it was in his handwriting. Prately replied that it might be'. This letter, it transpired, had been written in prison and almost smuggled out inside another letter. It had been intercepted. Dated 20th March and addressed to 'Dearest Joe', it was, judging by the content, obviously intended for the writer's wife. It read:

'I want to say a few things that is best said now as later on, but you need not let them worry you, as the expected must be looked at. When I start my trail, it is not unlikely that I may be sentenced to death,and it is best to know now instead of coming as a shock later on. This letter is being slipped out. It would be better to burn it in case it comes into the hands of the police. No matter how the case goes, I hope the two men who were with me will do their best for you. I don't mention names, as it is best not to, you know what I mean. 'I may want you to give something to a woman to bring in, as you could not bring it in yourself. I may not want it. In case I do, I will write through the same source next week. After the trial comes off, I am going to say that I changed guns with one of the others as his gun was to big to go into his pocket. That was how I had that particular gun in my pocket.'

(Pratley had also been committed for trial in connection with another murder, but charges were later dropped against him.)

After sentence of death was passed on him, Pratley maintained an outward show of calm; and, right up to the very end, protected the identity of his two accomplices. Indeed, he even said he was glad they had escaped, and wished them luck. He was visited by relatives every day. On the morning of Pratley's execution, the usual crowd (numbering about 2000) gathered outside the prison gates. Their patience was rewarded when, a few minutes after eight, the usual official notices were posted, stating that the justice had been done etc. It was signed by the Under-Sheriff and the prison's governor, doctor and chaplain. Two warders had attended Prately at all times in his cell, right from the very moment he had been placed under sentence of death. That morning, he rose early but refused breakfast. Fathers McGouran and Wall visited him after he dressed, and went with him to another cell, in which a temporary altar had been set up. Mass was celebrated. Pratley devoutly made the responses and received the last rites of the Roman Catholic Church. He was then removed to a cell adjoining the scaffold. Willis, with 86 'hangings' already under his belt, was assisted by Wilson. Pratley offered no resistance when these two pinioned him in his cell. Supported by the warders, and accompanied by the priests reciting the burial service prayer and officials, Pratley set off on his last walk. Within seconds of leaving his cell, Prately was dead, executed in the clothes he had worn at his trail. After the body had hung for an hour, it was cut down. The clergymen conducted another service. The remains were inspected by the City Coroner (Dr. James Graham), who held an inquest without a jury. Pratley was then interred within the prison's walls.

The Execution of William Smiley
on 8th August 1928

Smiley was described as an exemplantry prisoner,who was an ex-
serviceman, and a married man with a family. Since he was sentenced he had been under the guard of warders night and day. He
gave no trouble, but he held out little hope of a reprieve, and was
visited by his wife, for whose welfare he was greatly concerned.
Smiley had been charged with and sentenced for the brutal murder
of the Misses Sarah and Margaret McCauley at their farm house,
Mullaghduff, near Armoy, County Antrim. The trial was held at the
County Antrim Assizes Belfast, before the Lord Chief Justice on the
10th July 1928. The case attracted a considerable amount of public
interest. Punctually at 10.30 his Lordship took his seat on the bench
and the clerk of the court called to the jail governor for the production of William Smiley. In the dock there was an immediate move-
ment and Smiley appeared in view between two warders. He
stepped briskly forward and after a hasty glance round the court
stood to attention with hands rigid by the legs in approved military
fashion. Smiley was attired in a closely buttoned suit of serge cloth
and in place of a collar wore a white muffler which was neatly
pinned over his chest. He pleaded not guilty in a clear tone when
arraigned by the clerk. On the solicitor's table was a scale model of
the farm house of the Maculeys where the tragedy was enacted.
Relatives of the deceased ladies and of the accused were provided
with seating accommodation in various parts of the court. It took a
full twenty five minutes in obtaining a jury. In the end twelve jurors
were sworn in. The Attorney General, A.B. Babington (K.C/M.P.)
MrDavidson (K.C./M.P.) and Mr. Shields instructed by Mussen the
Crown Solicitor appeared to prosecute and the accused was defended by Mr Frederick H. Charles. Prisoner was first put on trial
with the indictment that he on the 24th May 1928 feloniously
wilfully and of his malice afore thought did kill and murder one
Margaret McCauley. The Attorney General opened the case for the
Crown. During his speech Smiley set in the dock immovable except
for the occasional twitching being the only indication that the was
closely following the case being built up against him. He glanced
now and then in the direction of the jury, but for the most part looked
steadfastly in front of him. It was stated that the wife of the accused

64

was in court and presented a pathetic figure. A murder of revolting horror and brutality was how the Attorney General described the crime at the opening of his address. He said the evidence that would be submitted against the prisoner Smiley was circumstantial, that was to say, no human eye saw the murder actually committed but the evidence, although circumstantial the crown would submit was absolutely conclusive. The Attorney General then proceeded to deal with the evidence in detail and invited the jury to follow him closely in his recital of the facts. The place where the murder took place was in a house at Mullaghduff which was about two miles from Armoy, and in that house resided the Macauley's, which consisted of Mr. Andrew McCauley who was a well know farmer and a justice of the peace and chairman of Ballycastle rural District Council, his brother Mr. Leslie McCauley and the two sisters, Miss Margaret and Sarah McCauley. The four Macauleys lived in the house together, and the brothers having a large farm of 300 acres and the two sisters assisted in the general work of the house. The family had by way of assistance two farm labourers Thomas McCaughan and the prisoner William Smiley. McCaughan lived in Armoy, and the prisoner who was married lived about a quarter of a mile away. The family had also a general worker about the place a woman called Kate Murdock whose evidence was of very great importance. The McCauley family, said the Attorney General, was well to do and highly respected and lived in a peaceful agricultural community, into this peaceful scene on the 24th May inst. grim murder stalked, cunning, cruel and callous. Between the hours of 12.30 and 1.15 the two sisters were murdered at home. The Attorney General then described the movements of the family upon the day of the murder which was a Thursday, in the early part of that day Mr. Andrew McCauley and his brother Leslie went out to work upon a fence about three-quarters of a mile away from his own home. The prisoner Smiley and his fellow worker McCaughan went out to plough in a field convenient to the house. At this stage the Attorney General produced a large map showing the McCauley's house and other points mentioned in his statement. Copies of these were handed to the judge and jury. The Attorney General said McCauley house was reached from the main road by a short laneway which went downhill. He explained where the McCauley brothers were working at the fence and said this was about three-quarters of a mile from the house. This would be told by witnesses that it took about twenty-five minutes to walk from McCauley's house to the fence. It was a falling country and there was a clear view of the house and the avenue leading down from it to the main road. Council also pointed out the main road where Smiley and McCaughan were working. Convenient to this field was the house of a man named McLarnon who would be examined in the case. He also referred the jury to the two fields in which the McCauley's cattle had been grazed. On that day the cattle were taken out of one field by Kate Murdock and brought down to be watered and finally taken back to another field. All of which were largely down on the highway close to the lane. Coming to events immediately before the murder council said that in or about 11.30 on that morning Sarah McCauley started from her home to take dinner to where her brothers were working at the fence. It would take her twenty to twenty five minutes to reach them and she would arrive there about 12 o'clock. The times are all important. Sarah arrived about 12 o'clock to where the brothers were working working and remained until they had finished, both McCauley brothers would tell them that about 12.30, finishing dinner she parcelled up the remains and started back home. Council said she would arrive normally at 12.45 or 1 o'clock but probably about five minutes to one. The Attorney General then dealt with events at the house and said that ten minutes to twelve, the dinner hour of the family apparently about noon, Kate Murdock was called in to dinner by Miss Margaret McCauley. Murdock had been working behind the house budding potatoes. McCaughan and Smiley loosed their horses in the field and came in for dinner, McCaughan would tell them that they came in about twenty minutes to twelve and that he saw Miss Sarah on her way down to where her brothers were working. The two men came in and after putting in their horses they entered the house a few minutes before twelve o'clock. There were then in the house the two men Smiley and McCaughan, Miss Margaret and Kate Murdock. They sat down to dinner together and the jury would be told that while they were having the meal Miss Margaret was sitting at the end of the table reading a newspaper and by an extraordinary coincidence the subject matter of the article she was reading to the prisoner and the other two workers was the Cutteridge murder which some of the jury would probably recall. Kate Murdock was the first to leave the kitchen she having been told to go out and bring in a basket of peat, while she was filling her basket the prisoner and McCaughan came out of the house and went round the stables, at about twenty minutes past twelve McCaughan had arranged to go off for the afternoon and when he and the prisoner got round to the stable he said to Smiley I am off now and reached for his coat. The prisoner then asked him to give his horse a drink and McCaughan told them he had done so. McCaughan then got his coat and bicycle and went out of the farm yard wheeling his machine and as he was leaving Smiley said to him, "see and take care of yourself". McCaughan further told them that as he was going out of the yard Smiley was then walking in the direction of the stable with corn to give the horses a feed and he would further tell them it would take the horses half an hour to complete the feed. It was about 12.30 when McCaughan left the yard and he did not mount his bicycle until he met the main road. As he passed the kitchen door of the house Miss Margaret McCauley called to him, and as he was going down the avenue he saw at that time Sarah McCauley away in the distance over the fence where her brothers were working, she was then leaving for home. This would corroborate the story told by the McCauley brothers themselves and council added in passing that all the times in the case fitted in almost to a fraction of a minute. McCaughan also saw Kate Murdock taking the cattle out of the field to give them a drink and she was bringing them along the road. The Attorney General then traced the movements of Kate Murdock who took the cattle out of the field to give a drink and brought them back to another field. This would take about half an hour, it would be shown she was finished about one o'clock. By this time Miss Sarah had walked from where the brothers were working, to the house and they would reach the lane about the same moment. Council added that the time was pretty well fixed because while Kate Murdock was on the road working with the cattle. Sergt. Connolly who is in charge of Armoy Barracks with another policemen was cycling towards Armoy in the ordinary course of duty and he passed her on the road about a quarter to one. The Attorney General then said that Kate Murdock and Sarah Macualey who was returning from the field walked up the avenue to the house together, Kate Murdock had a stick with her which she had been using to drive the cattle, and she handed this to her sister, this was about one o'clock, Kate Murdock went round to the back of the house to complete her work and did not see Sarah go into the house. One thing was certain that within a few minutes the Crown could not fix the time with absolute precision after Miss Sarah came back with Kate Murdock, for she was shot dead in her own house. This occurred between 1.00 and 1.15. A little while after Kate Murdock had gone to the back of the house she heard a shot quite plain and quite clear. She got up and looked around but saw nobody and paid little attention to it because there was a gun in the house and Andrew and sometimes the prisoner used the gun to shoot the crows. Smiley had actually used the gun a few days before for shooting crows. Beyond all doubt said the Attorney General, that shot was the shot that killed Miss Sarah. Who fired it? That was one matter the jury would have to consider. Where was the prisoner at this time? At five to ten past one he was on the premises. He was the only living soul upon the premises with the exception of Sarah and Kate Murdock because as they would hear later on Margaret at that time lay down having been shot at an earlier period when there was nobody on the premises to hear the shot and when the door of the house was in all probability closed. There was one thing that would be made absolutely plain in the case mainly that the prisoner did not take his horses out again after McCaugan had left at 12.30, and did not take them out actually until after this shot heard by Kate Murdock which had been fired about twenty five past one. Kate Murdock would tell then that some little time after the shot she heard the sound of horses feet. The roadway was cobbled and the Crown would summit that that noise was the prisoner taking out the horse. The murder of these two ladies was seen by no mortal eye. Dealing with the statement made by the prisoner the Attorney General said that Smiley, on the 24th May, stated to Sergeant Connolly that he took the horses out immediately after McCaugan left. That was to say at 12.30. All the evidence would prove to them conclusively that that was not so. Of course the prisoner had a very great interest in getting himself off the premises at 12.30 because up to that hour or a few minutes before it Miss Margaret was alive, council said there would be evidence form Mr. Leslie McCauley who actually saw with his own eyes the horses being taken out about twenty five past one. He was watching for the horses to come as the result of a conversation he had with Smiley in the morning as to what horses he was going to use that afternoon. In additionto this there was another witness, M'Larnon, who lived in a house next door to the field in which Smiley was working who would prove that Smiley went into the field at 1.30. Kate Murdock would also tell them that she was on the road from shortly before 12.30 and that the prisoner could not have got into the field without her seeing him. Therefore the prisoner must have been on the premises council said. Smiley made another statement at the inquest in which he stated he left the field about a quarter past one. Obviously the prisoner had found it difficult to reconcile his movements upon that day on the evidence of the Crown. The murder of the sisters had been completed at a quarter past one and he suggested that Smiley's earlier story was wrong. Dealing with the discovery of the murder, council said that at about three o'clock Kate Murdock having finished her work went round to the kitchen door and entered. The spectacle presented was almost too horrible for belief. Both the sisters were lying dead in a pool of blood with most wounds inflicted by a gun. Miss Margaret apparently was murdered first and council said that every fact and every circumstances in the case points to the prisoner and to the prisoner alone as being the man that had committed these murders. The Attorney General next drew the attention of the jury to the model of the McCauley dwelling and pointed out the main features particularly in relation to the kitchen and the furnishing of the apartment. He then indicated the evidence that would be produced as to the discovery of the bodies, and said in the case of Margaret there were indications that the muzzle had been quite close to the victim when the gun was fired. A salt box was lying under her right arm and salt was scattered over the floor, across her body lay a double barrelled gun with a spent cartridge. The injuries sustained by Sarah would go to show she was shot from a longer range and he (the Attorney General) suggested her assailant fired from a place of concealment. There was no sign of the kitchen having been ransacked but there were such indications in a bedroom and also in the loft. The sum of thirty pounds in ten pound notes, six half crowns and five shilling pieces were missing. Also a gold watch. The gun, said Mr.Babington was kept on a beam and the box ammunition was nearby. It was plain, said the Attorney General, that the murderer must have taken down the gun in the presence of Margaret McCauley who was engaged in her domestic duties in the kitchen. He must have taken the cover off and having laid it down on the couch he must have opened the ammunition box. He loaded the gun in her presence without rousing any suspicion or alarm that she would naturally feel if a stranger did this. She was going about her work in the ordinary way. Near the table there was the bake board and she had a salt box under her arm. At that moment she was shot behind the right ear. Who could have completed that transaction but the prisoner. Council drew the attention to the jury that whereas the body of Margaret was cold when discovered that of Sarah was warm which showed Sarah was done to death after her sister. The Crown suggested Margaret was shot shortly after 12.30 and then no one heard the shot which was due to the fact the door was shut. The miscreant then proceeded to rifle the house and while doing this he was disturbed by the arrival of Sarah about one o'clock or shortly after. As she entered her house Sarah would see the body of her sister. Of that there could be no question and he (council) thought the second crime could be reconstructed without much difficulty. The murderer of Margaret heard the approach of Sarah and as she opened the door he stepped back through another door and as Sarah walked towards her sister to see what had happened he (the Intruder) fired at Sarah, practically blowing her head off. The Attorney General said there could be no doubt that the motive was robbery and he next briefly reviewed the statement made by the accused to the police as to his movements and also as to his statement that after reporting the tragedy to the police he went to a public house in Armoy and there had whiskey. He told the police while in the public house he heard someone talking about the raid. Evidence would be called that there was no one in the public house and council suggested that the voices existed only in the imagination of one who was in a state of nervous apprehension arising from the commission of a crime. Mr. Babington then related to the jury how the District Inspector and Sergeant Connolly went to the house of the accused, which was a quarter of a mile away and there received a suit of clothes which were taken to the barracks and while changing into them accused remarked to Constable Whiteman that one of the socks was rather thick. The constable then examined the boot and found in the toe some paper which proved to be three ten pounds notes which Mr McCauley had in his cash box in the bedroom. Prisoner when he saw the notes said, ' have you got it all, there should be thirty pounds I got it when I was with Leslie it was lying on the floor. I was up seeing if it was all right.' Then, said council, prisoner made an indecent remark suggesting he did not care what happened. Concluding his summing address which had occupied ninety minutes the Attorney General said, the chain of circumstances was absolute. There was not a gap in it and there was not a point in doubt when they came to contrast it with the story told by the accused. The first witness was Sergeant R. Brown, head of the photographic and finger print department, R.U.C., who produced a map of the vicinity of the McCauley household and in answer to (M) Division, gave measurements. He also supposed that the model produced was constructed to scale. There was no upper storey and there was only one entrance, i.e. that into the kitchen. Inside the kitchen into the parlour, was a drop of four and a half inches. From the parlour, there was access to a passage in which a ladder led to a room over the parlour. This room was in the newer portion of the building. The witness pointed out the beam in the kitchen on which the gun was kept, and also the shelf where the cartridge box was usually placed.

Mr Campbell (cross examination) did you take any fingerprints in this case? Witness - I did. Did you give them in evidence at any stage? Witness - No. Have you given finger print evidence in other Crown prosecutions? Witness - I have.

In answer to further questions, witness said there were hedges along the main road in front of the avenue. There was a cluster of trees and the road rose very sharply. The nearest dwelling house to the Macauley's was 150 or 160 yards distance.

Mr. Davidson (in examination) what finger prints did you take? Witness - I got some finger marks on a cash box, I compared them with the finger marks of the prisoner, and found they were not his, I then inquired as to who had handled the box. Mr. Campbell K.C. - I object my Lord. Mr. Davidson, did you take the finger prints of any other persons? Witness - Yes. I had finger prints of the police who had handled the cash box. His Lordship - When was this? Witness - 22nd June. Mr. Davidson - Were you able to identify finger prints on the cash box? Witness - I was. What were they? Witness - Four by Sergeant Connolly and one by Head Constable Cromie. You were able to identify all the finger prints you saw on the cash box? Witness - I was. Were there other marks on the box? Witness - Yes, finger marks pulled and superimposed. I could make nothing of them. Were you able to identify any of Macauley's finger prints? Witness- I was not.

His Lordship - I suppose the cash box was produced at the inquest and handled there.

Kate Murdock, a domestic servant in the employment of McCauley's stated that on the day of the tragedy she was at work at the back of the house budding potatoes. She left off about ten to twelve and went to the kitchen, where she saw Miss McCauley, also Smiley and

71

McCaugan. They sat down to dinner with the exception of Maggie McCauley, who was on the sofa reading a newspaper. What was she reading about?asked the Attorney General. Witness - A murder. What was the name?There was the name Brown I remember. You have one name right anyhow. How long did it take you to finish your dinner?--Twenty minutes. Witness said she left the table first about 12.20 and went out to get a basket of peat. As she returned she met the prisoner and McCaugan leaving the kitchen. She went to attend cattle and to take them a drink. When witness was down she saw Sergeant Connolly, who was going to Armoy. Witness also saw Sarah who was coming from her brothers, approaching the road. When Sarah came up to the road the pair of them stood for two or three minutes and then went up the little avenue to the house. Witness had a stick with her and give it to Sarah to give it to Maggie. Witness left Sarah at the house again. Witness did not see Sarah actually enter. When she was at work some time later she heard a shot . His Lordship - How long had you been working when you heard the shot? The witness - It was a very short time. Witness explained she did not take any particular notice of the shot. She got up and looked around, but saw nobody. Two or three minutes after the shot she heard the sound of horse's feet. The horses were at the front of the house and then went round to the house. She opened the door and called but got no response. She then went in and saw the two sisters lying in their blood with a gun beside them. Witness rushed down to the road and told a man with a horse and cart what had happened. He told her to go and tell Smiley who was working in the field. Witness told Smiley, who said, "It could not be." Witness replied it was true. Smiley then went up to the house and came down again on a bicycle. As he passed her he said that God had been good to her, and that if she had been near the house she would have been shot too. Witness stated that she never saw Smiley from the time he left the house after dinner and when she was down watering cattle. She did not see Smiley in the field, and if he had appeared anywhere she would have seen him. Witness did not go to the second field with the cattle but remained for about five minutes talking to Sarah. Then she went on to the house, she did not think it was an hour from the time she met the Sergeant until she reached the house. The gun was lying on the floor at Sarah's side. Witness did not look close as she was upset .

Mr. Davidson replied for the Crown, and suggested that the man

72

who committed the crime was no ordinary man, but someone cunning and callous. First he had to kill Margaret and then her sister. Mr Campbell had suggested that Smiley, who pretended to be helping Leslie McCauley to look for the money, actually took the thirty pounds with the sisters dead on the floor below. Robbery was the motive for the crime and contended the blunder was found in Smiley's boot. It was a good hiding place and but for a chance it would never have been discovered.

His Lordship proceeded to sum up at 8.35. He said, at the outset that after the exhaustive addresses of council he need say little more than to assist the jury in arriving at a conclusion. He did not think there was any doubt as to the motive. It was robbery whoever did it. If it was proved that the prisoner was the only person in or about the premises there was robbery. A sum of thirty pounds disappeared and that amount was found in possession of the prisoner. In the absence of explanations and there being no evidence or suggestions of any other person or persons in the vicinity, it was for the prisoner to show how he came properly by the money independent of the crime. It rested with the prisoner, once he was found in possession of the stolen money, the proceeds of a robbery, to show how he came by it. The question was did he get the money at the time the murder was committed, or after the murder was discovered. In this opinion, no satisfactory explanation had been given. The explanation as to possession of the money was a matter for the jury to decide. His Lordship referred to the evidence of Mrs Smiley and said he always, had the greatest sympathy with wives who came forward in an endeavour to save husbands from the consequence of crime. Her evidence was given in a very straightforward manner. The question for the jury was did they believe the prisoner or his wife or the McCauley's and the police and the other witness called by the Crown? If the jury thought there was a reasonable doubt, they must give the prisoner the benefit of it. If there was no doubt, then the prisoner would have to pay the penalty for one of the most barbarous and brutal murders that had happened in their time and generation in this country.

Less than a quarter of an hour was taken by the jury in the Armoy murder case to reach their verdict, into a hushed court with eye's upon them, the jurors filed from their consulting room. The clerk then asked Smiley if he had anything to say? Smiley, who was slightly paler but still a firm figure in the dock, replied in a loud voice, "I am innocent of the murder." Not a sound was heard in the court after this, but the dread words of the death sentence. Every eye was on the judge, who in a few tense words sent Smiley to his doom. His Lordship, in passing the sentence of death, said Smiley had been tried by a jury of his peers. He had been ably defended by learned council. Every consideration had been given to the case and the jury had arrived in his opinion, at the only conclusion which any fair minded jury could arrive at, mainly, that he was guilty of murder. I do not wish to say anything to increase the melancholy circumstances in which you stand here, added his Lordship. You gave these unfortunate women no chance, not a moment before you hurled them into eternity. The law is more merciful to you because you are to be afforded some period in which to make peace with your maker. I now pass upon you the dreadful sentence and judgment of the court. His Lordship assumed the black cap, and sentenced Smiley to be hanged on 8th August. Smiley, received the sentence unmoved, and, except for a slight change of colour, was taken below. It was interesting that all through his trail that he showed no remorse but just before he was hung he admitted his guilt of the crime. Pierpoint was the executioner and Baxter was his assistant. It was a matter of seconds only from the time the condemned man stepped from the cell to the scaffold. The eyewitnesses who were present at the final stage were impressed with the cool manner in which Smiley bore himself, and it stated that he went to his death smiling.

"Duly executed by being hanged by the neck until death as required by law" was the verdict returned by the City Coroner (Dr, James Graham), who held the inquest after the execution. The governor of the prison, Major Long, gave evidence that Smiley was committed on the 26th May charged with the murder, and on July the 10th he was convicted and sentenced to death. At 8 o'clock that morning the Under-Sheriff for the county Antrim had taken him over for the execution. Dr. O'Flaherty, (Medical Officer of the gaol) who was present at the hanging, said death, which was instantaneous, was due to the dislocation of the neck.

The Execution of Samuel Cushnahan
on 8th April 1930

Samuel Cushnahan, a twenty-six-year-old farm labourer from county Antrim, was hanged on the 8th April 1930 for the murder of a postman on his way to Crosskeys Post Office. Robbery was the motive.

Cushnahan was first tried at the Winter Assizes in Londonderry, but the jury failed to agree. He stood trail again at the Spring Assizes in Belfast and was sentenced to death. Cushnahan, defended by Mr. W.Lowery, KC, and Mr. J. Campbell, (instructed by Mr J Taylor, Ballymena). He pleaded "not guilty."

Ten jurors had been ordered to 'stand by' , and there were ten challenges on behalf of the prisoner; it took half-an-hour to swear in a jury. Opening the case for the crown, the Attorney General, the Rt. Hon. A. Babington, KC, told the crowded courthouse that the accused, Samuel Cushnahan, stood charged with the wilful murder of Mr. James McCann on 16th May.

The Attorney General said he would not go into all the evidence, only the parts which were of importance pro and contra the defendant. No-one had witnessed the murder, he said, but supposing that a cap with the defendant's name on it had been found at the scene of the crime? What inference would one drew from that? Would one not say that the wearer was somehow mixed up with the crime? No cap had been found at the scene of the crime; a scrap of cloth had, though. It could not be proved that this scrap of cloth was from the defendant's coat, but the evidence said that the scrap was from the same loom as the cloth of the defendant's coat. Had the jury any satisfactory explanation as to how this scrap came to be found at the scene of the crime? If not, then this scrap was a damning piece of evidence against the defendant. It would be the most natural thing in the world, would it not, the prosecution went on, for the murderer to take to the back fields instead of going through the village of Milltown? A Mrs Brown had seen someone in those fields behind her home at a distance of two hundred yards. She had known Cushnahan from childhood, but could not say for sure whether or not it was the man in the dock she had seen. She could only say that the man was of small build, and wearing a dark coat and khai-coloured trousers. It was up to the jury to decide whether or not they thought that this man was Cushnahan. The prosecution itself considered this very probable.

As for a letter written by the defendant in jail, the prosecution, argued that a reference to a scythe was an illusion to the gun, and not to the missing barrel. It was an innocent letter; but, continued the prosecution, it was hard to see why, if this were the case, the defendant had found it necessary to do, if he wanted the weapon produced in court was to inform the governor or his solicitor. If, on the other hand, the jury was of the opinion that the 'scythe' was really the missing gun-barrel, then this was a very damning letter indeed. But it all depended on how the jury constructed the facts. As for the money, if Cushnahan had been referring to the calf-money, then it was a perfectly innocent letter; but if he had been referring to the Post Office pension money, then it was absolutely damning. It was up to the jury to decide. The defendant had two things in his favour; his previous good character, and the fact that no traces of blood had been found on his clothing. He, of course, protested his innocence, as did his brothers; he also denied that any interview with Mrs Robinson had taken place. Cushanan was, the prosecution concluded, entitled to the benefit of any reasonable doubt, but the jury could not invent doubt for him. "And now, gentlemen, may God's blessing rest on your oaths," the jury was told before retiring. The Lord Chief Justice left the bench; the prisoner was taken below to the cells. On the 8th March 1930, sentence was passed on Cushnahan. The jury had agreed unanimously that Cushnahan was guilty of wilful murder. Cushnahan was asked why sentence of death and execution should not be awarded against him and passed upon him, according to law. He answered in a voice that was scarcely audible: 'I have nothing to say,' The Lord Chief Justice then added:

'Samuel Cushnahan, a jury of your native county, on evidence that must have satisfied every man, have found you guilty of the terrible crimes of murder of your fellow citizen, and no-one can say that their verdict was not fully justified. I concur in it, and I thank the jury, who have performed a painful duty and have found the only verdict that they could. My duty now is (putting on the black cap) to pass the dreadful sentence of the law . The sentence and judgment of the court are and it is hereby ordered and adjured that you, Samuel Cushnahan, to be taken from the bar of this court in which you now stand to the prison from which you came, and that on Tuesday 8th April in the same year of our Lord 1930 you be taken to the common place of execution in the jail in which you are now confined, and then and there be hanged by the neck until you are dead, and that your body be buried within the walls of the prison in which the aforesaid judgment of death shall have been executed uponyou. And may the lord have mercy on your soul.'

The condemned man immediately turned and walked unaided to the rear of the dock and down the stairway to the underground passage leading from the courthouse to the prison.

Unsuccessful attempts to secure a reprieve for Cushnahan were made in the weeks before his execution. On the morning of 8th April crowds gathered in the cold and rain outside the prison on Belfast's Crumlin Road. The condemned man's mother and father, as well as other relatives were among them, His mother in particular cut a most pathetic figure, grasping the iron railings to support herself, and bowing her head on her breast.

By 3 am the crowd had swollen to several hundred . Some knelt before the gates, produced rosaries and began to pray. At the stroke of eight women began singing: 'Jesus Lord, I ask for mercy,; 'Ave Maria'; and' Star of the sea'.

Cushnahan had been attended to spiritually by fathers Mc Gournan and Walls, prison chaplains. They said later that their charge had died with great Christian Courage and charity, Pierpont was the executioner, assisted by Wilis.

The inquests into all other hangings we have examined so far involved juries. In this case there was none. The inquest began at 10 am. Graham was the City Coroner at the time. It was a formality. Cushnahan was interred within the prison grounds.

The Execution of Thomas Dornan
on 31st July 1931

Thomas Dornan, a farmer, was hanged at the age of 41 for the murder of two sisters. Bella and Margaret Aiken had lived on a farm near Dornan. He shot them as they worked in a bog at Newtowncrommelin near Ballymena on 23rd May 1931. The murders took place in broad daylight and was witnessed by a number of people in the immediate vicinity.

The murders seem to have been an act of revenge on the part of a man ruminating on an imaginary slight over an irksome financial burden. Dornan, a married man, was described as industrious, and was held in high regard as a respectable member of the local community. He was on friendly terms with the Aiken family, who were also highly regarded in the area. A friendship grew between Dornan and Bella, the younger of the two sisters at 20, and before long she gave birth to an illegitimate child; Dornan admitted to being the father and agreed to pay 6s a week in support of the child.

By the time of the murders he had already paid a total of over £18, but it appears that he had fallen behind with his payments. His penultimate payment had been made in the middle of January and the final one was not made until 26th March, two months before the central event in this account.

At the trial, the Crown stressed premeditation. On the afternoon of the crime Dornan had walked to the bog, had a look around him without saying a word, and then walked home again to fetch a loaded shotgun. His pockets also contained cartridges. Dornan approached the girls calmly and shot them. He then strolled home, stopping once to tell a woman what he had just done.

He was soon arrested and tried before the Lord Chief Justice and a jury at the County Antrim Assizes on 8th July 1931. The Attorney General presented the Crown case with his customary forensic skill. Dornan was defended by Mr William Lowry K.C. and Mr J.M. Sparran B.L. was called.

Medical experts suggested that Dornan was not responsible for his actions and suffered from an uncontrollable homicidal impulse.

The jury listened carefully and returned a verdict of guilty after an absence of 32 minutes. Sentence of death was duly passed on Dornan.

On the morning of the execution spectators assembled outside H.M.P. Belfast on the Crumlin Road and were marshalled by the police. An ominous hush fell as the time set for the execution drew near, the tense silence punctuated only by the noise of a passing tram-car every now and then. Within ten minutes of the hanging the customary notice was posted on the gates of the prison. It stated that the condemned man had been visited by his wife, two sisters-in-law and their husbands. They had been with him for two hours.

It had been a distressing final interview but Dornan had assured them that he was reconciled to his fate. The Rev Simms had visited Dornan three times a day and found him very penitent. A change, apparently, had come over Dornan, who had sought solace in religion. Dornan had thanked the warders for their kindness and walked briskly to the scaffold with his head held high and prayed shortly before Pierrepoint and his assistant, Wilson, did their job.

The Turk Murder
The Execution of Eddie Cullens
on 13th January 1932

It was a morning like any other for James McCalmont. He was up with the dawn and had done two hours' chores on the farm by nine o'clock. Now he hitched the horse to the cart, loaded it with milk churns, and set off down the lane to the main road.

But in that quiet country lane the morning ceased to be like any other. It was one James McCalmont would never forget. Nor would the people of Carrickfergus.

For the autumn fields of Seskin the first act in a fantastic drama was about to be played ..... a crime story which stands as Ulster's strangest.

It was James's horse that first sensed danger. It plodded quietly along the familiar lane until it came to a cornfield bordered by a dry stone wall where it stopped, whinnied with fear, and started to back away. James McCalmont tried to control the horse but could not; the horse would not be coaxed to go any further. James got off the cart and looked around to see what had startled the animal. Behind the wall, in the lonely cornfield, he found the reason ..... a dead boy.

The discovery of any corpse is a shock but this one was grotesque. It was that of a big man, sprawled on his back ..... wearing nothing but a lady's bathing-cap. The left eye stared emptily at the sky and the right was tightly closed in an obscene wink. Under it was a tiny puncture wound.

Within an hour the cornfield was swarming with policemen. Photographs of the body were taken and preliminary examinations carried out by police doctors. C.I.D. chiefs from Belfast arrived, then reporters. By evening everyone in Northern Ireland was reading about the 'Mystery at Carrickfergus.'

The fact that the body was naked and that a bathing-cap had been pulled tightly over its head, after death, was bizarre enough, but more sensations were to come.

Even the formal police description of the dead man read strangely: 'about 35 years of age, height 6' 2", brown eyes, black hair, high cheekbones, Roman nose slightly turned to the side, large mouth with thick lips, very irregular teeth, slight burn marks about 2" under the left ear, very dark swarthy skin, muscular build, somewhat flat feet. The man is of Jewish or foreign appearance.'

The mystery corpse was discovered on 4th September 1931 and for nineteen days its identity puzzled the police. How had this dark foreign giant met his death in the quiet Carrickfergus countryside? Who was he? Where did he come from? Ulster buzzed with rumours. Patient detectives investigated every theory, no matter how unlikely.

One story was that the dead man was a member of a hold-up gang which had raided a bank in Scotland some weeks before and that he had been 'rubbed out' by his fellow thieves. Even more melodramatic was the story that he was an expatriate Russian tracked down and liquidated by agents of the Kremlin. When the real story of the murder, however, was unravelled, it was even more fantastic than the wildest of the rumours. It was a story which began in Turkey and moved to New York and London; a tale which led detectives to the big top of Bertram Mills's Circus and to an earthen-floored garage in Liverpool.

The inquest on the body was opened in Carrickfergus on 6th September, and on the flimsy evidence available a formal open verdict was returned. The only facts about which the police could be sure were that the man was not known in the area ..... and that he had been shot twice in the head by a .25 automatic pistol. They were also sure that the mystery man had not been murdered in the cornfield; his body had been dumped there some time later.

Over the next fortnight more scraps of evidence came to light. In a gateway off Church Lane in Belfast a bundle of clothes was found. There was a blue waterproof coat from which the sleeves had been ripped, a bloodstained jacket, and a pair of trousers slashed from waist to turn-ups. Were these the clothes of the dead man, cut from his body by his killer?

The following day a man's shoe was found. It was a size ten from which the tongue had been cut. Police switched their inquiries to Belfast's dockland and interviewed the crews of all visiting foreign ships, knowing that it was common practice among seamen to mark their shoes by writing their names on the tongues.

Some witnesses told the police that they had seen a big foreign-looking man in Customs House Square in Belfast on 28th August. He had been accompanied by a 'dapper little man in a beret.'

After a week public interest in the strange killing began to dwindle and it looked as if the Carrickfergus case would end up in the 'unsolved crimes' file. But on 21st September newspapers carried a small item stating that District Inspector Lewis and Head Constable Black of C.I.D. had gone to London for consultations with Scotland Yard detectives in connection with the Carrick murder and the next day the real story broke. It was a story which kept Ulster talking for the next three months.

The two top detectives had traced the tenuous clues to a circus in Leeds where they showed the grotesque pictures of the Carrickfergus corpse to roustabouts in Bertram Mill's Circus. They identified the corpse as one Achmed Musa, a hanger-on with one of the sideshows. Within a few hours the Belfast investigators had almost solved the crime. They found the murder weapon .... and the prime suspect, a man called Eddie Cullens. Three months later Cullens was executed in Belfast Prison for the crime which came to be known throughout Northern Ireland as the 'Turk Murder.'

It all began in Istanbul. Musa, a drifter with a talent for making easy money, was temporarily out of funds and looking for a new racket. Following up a rumour, he went to a village near the Turkish capital and found there his new meal-ticket, an old man called Zara Agha who claimed to be 156 years of age. Musa persuaded the old man to come back to Istanbul with him and sought out one Assim Redvan. Excitedly he outlined his plan: if Redvan, a showman, would put up the money, they could exhibit Agha in America as 'The Oldest Man in the World.'

A month later the Turkish trio arrived in New York. The American showbiz-men they contacted were not very interested in the stunt and the Turks grew desperate. Assim Redvan was the only member of the party who spoke English. Anxiously he made contacts, searching for an opening which would lead him to the fringes of the New York underworld .... and to Eddie Cullens.

Cullens was a cinema projectionist with vague connections to small-time vaudeville shows. He was a native of Cyprus who had emigrated to the States as a teenager and become a naturalised citizen.

When Assim approached him, Cullens offered a deal: 'Cut me in as a full partner in the syndicate and I will use my connections to get the old man into a show.' The Turks had no option. They agreed and, good as his word, Cullens persuaded a carnival to exhibit Agha. He also arranged to have pictures of the old man taken and printed and the sale of these added to the group's revenue.

In June 1931 the strange syndicate sailed from New York to London. Assim and Cullens arranged a meeting with Bertram Mills's Circus and, to their great delight, the big touring show accepted Zara Agha as part of the company. The deal was that Agha would be employed as a performer with Assim as his personal manager. Musa and Cullens, while not on the Circus payroll, would share in the money paid by the other two.

For a while things went quite well. 'The Oldest Man in the World' was a success in the Circus and the partners prospered. In August, however, squabbling broke out. Cullens and Musa decided to try their luck with something else. When the circus reached Wavertree, a suburb of Liverpool, Cullens told Assim that he wanted to tour around the country and asked the Turk to lend him his car. He agreed. Musa then approached Assim and told him he was joining Cullens and needed money. Assim lent him £30, holding Musa's Post Office Savings book (he had £67 in his account) as security.

On 28th August the two booked the car, a cream and brown Essex, and took the boat to Belfast, arriving the following morning.

That is the story so far. Strange though it is, it becomes stranger .... and more sinister. For as a County Armagh jury would later hear, Eddie Cullens had more than a holiday in mind when he cane to Belfast. He had already decided to kill Musa.

The most baffling aspect of the whole Turk case is that no-one has ever discovered a motive for Cullen's crime. Why did he kill Musa? It could not have been for the few pounds the Turk was carrying on him. And it was not a surge of sudden anger. The killing of Achmed Musa was cleverly planned and coldbloodedly executed.

At the three-day trial the prosecution did not even attempt to establish a motive for the murder. The Lord Chief Justice told the jury in his summing-up that they need not worry about that aspect. 'How can we tell what animated these men?' he asked. 'We do not know what lay between them, but if Cane kills Abel, it does not matter on what grounds. Murder has been committed and the blood cries out. It is immaterial for what purpose the murder is committed.'

One theory is that Cullen's motive was greed: he was dissatisfied with his cut of the circus money and got rid of Musa to increase his share of the takings from 'The Oldest Man in the World.'

The story of the arrival of the Turk-murderer in Northern Ireland was first told at a special court in Carrickfergus on 22nd September

1931. Huge crowds had gathered around the courthouse to watch the strange little man arrive under heavy police guard.

As Mr H.H. Mussen, the Crown Solicitor, opened his case, laughter and shouting could be heard from outside and the police were sent to disperse the crowd.

Mr Mussen said that Musa and Cullens had gone to a lodging house in Donegall Quay owned by a Mr and Mrs Ryan; they booked in for an indefinite stay.

That day, a Saturday, Cullens had driven Musa around Belfast in the big Essex car. The Turk's only hobby was chasing women, and within hours in the city he had found a 'friend.' Passing the Great Northern Railway Station in Great Victoria Street, Musa told Cullens to stop the car .... he had spotted a girl. She was Rose McGoldrick, later to be a star witness at the trial.

The car drew up beside her as she stepped from a telephone kiosk. The swarthy big Musa grinned at her and said something she could not understand. 'His English was very bad,' she recalled later, 'and the smaller man driving the car had to help him.' They asked her to go for a drive and she got into the car. Cullens later told the trial jury that they drove some way out of the city and he left Musa and the girl in the parked car for about half an hour. Cullens also said Musa paid Rose money. When they left her home it was arranged that they would meet her the following day and that Rose would bring along a friend to make up a foursome.

On Sunday morning the big Essex pulled up outside Belfast's General Post Office in Royal Avenue and Rose introduced her friend, Peggy Murphy, to the foreigners. They started out for Bangor but before they got very far the car developed a puncture. Cullens drove to a garage and asked to have the tyre repaired. The garage proprietor looked suspiciously at the strange foursome and told Cullens he could not mend the puncture on a Sunday.

Cullens was surprised by this answer but asked if he could change the wheel himself. The garage-owner agreed grudgingly.

While Musa and the two girls sat in the car talking, Cullens jacked up the axle and fitted the spare tyre. Then he went into the garage to wash his hands. As he returned to the car, shaking the water from his fingers, Rose leaned across and opened the door for him. Cullens reached into the glove compartment and pulled out a towel to dry his hands on. As he did so, something fell from the folds of the towel - a blue and white lady's bathing-cap. 'What do you keep that for?'

giggled Rose, reaching down to pick up the cap. 'Leave that alone,' snapped Cullens, 'keep your hands to yourself!' The girl was startled. But she decided to pull Cullens' leg a bit more. 'Aw, go on, what do you keep that for?' Stuffing the towel and the cap back into the glove compartment, Cullens grinned back at her, 'Oh, I wear that for my early-morning swim.'

They all laughed, then. But at the trial that little incident helped to put the noose around Cullens' neck. For the bathing-cap was the one later found on the head of the murdered Turk.

The two circus-men and the two Belfast girls spent the day in Bangor. Cullens was in good humour and kept chafing Musa about his meanness with money. The big Turk grew sullen.

On the way home Rose said that she had to visit relatives in Derry the next day, would Cullens drive her there? Musa was consulted and agreed. Cullens told Rose: 'Okay, but you needn't bring your friend Peggy along.'

On Monday 31st August, Musa and Cullens picked up Rose McGoldrick and drove to Derry. The little American was in expansive mood, bragging to Rose that he owned the big Essex car. 'It cost me £50 to bring it over from the States,' he boasted. Musa did not contradict him for he could not follow Cullens' rapid English and was too interested in gazing at the passing Ulster countryside.

At the trial Cullens said that when they reached Derry, Musa went off on his own and Rose went to see her friends. He arranged to meet them at 8 o'clock and decided to spend the day at the pictures. At 8 o'clock he met Musa again, but Rose did not turn up. They waited a few moments and then drove back to Belfast.

From the witness-box Cullens accused Rose McGoldrick of making up the story of seeing the bathing-cap because she was annoyed at being stranded in Derry.

The strange partners had established friendly relations with the Ryans. On Tuesday, the day after the Derry episode, Cullens took the couple out for a ride around Belfast. On the way back to Donegall Quay the car hit a tram and dented a mud wing. Cullens took it to James McIlroy's garage in Princes Street.

That night Mr Ryan, who was a bookmaker, invited Cullens and Musa to join him at Celtic Park Greyhound Track. They went to the garage to pick up the car. After they left, McIlroy noticed that his new blue waterproof coat was missing; he was later shown it, bloodstained and minus its sleeves, by the police. Unknown to

85

Cullens, Musa had stolen the coat while they were collecting the car from the garage. On the day of his death he had slipped it on ..... unwittingly providing the police with another damning piece of evidence against Cullens.

Cullens told Mrs Ryan the next Wednesday that he and his partner would be leaving her lodging-house that night. He settled the bills and waved goodbye to Mr Ryan who watched them drive off .... in the direction of Carrickfergus. It was the last time anyone was to see Achmed Musa alive. Next morning he was found shot dead in the Seskin cornfield.

Cullens' trial opened on 8th December 1931 in the high ceilinged Assize Court at Armagh. The Attorney General, Mr A.B. Babington, was brief in his opening address. He could afford to be for his array of witnesses provided an unanswerable case against Cullens.

Mr William Lowry K.C., led Cullens' defence, which was financed by some members of Belfast's Jewish community. He appealed to the jury's sympathy. Cullens, he said, was a foreigner 3000 miles from home, 'a stranger in a strange land,' depending on twelve County Armagh men for a fair trial.

The Belfast witnesses - Rose McGoldrick, Peggy Murphy, the Ryans, and garage-owner McIlroy all gave their evidence.

But then a new, and shocking, side of the case came to light. Witnesses from Liverpool and London gave evidence which pointed to Cullen as a calculating killer who had been planning the murder of his partner for more than a month.

Ben Carter, a Liverpool businessman, told the court that in early August Cullens, posing as 'Barney Berman,' called on him to rent a lock-up garage.

Cullens had asked him a curious question: what sort of floor did the garage have? When told it was of earth, Cullens said, 'That'll do.' A few days later, Mr Carter was passing the garage and heard sounds from inside. He tried the door, but found it was locked on the inside. He knocked and Cullens opened the door. 'He was hot and perspiring and was carrying a storm lantern. Propped against the garage wall was a pick and shovel.' This incident, claimed the prosecution, showed that Cullens was making clever preparations for a murder. He planned, they said, to bury the Turk in the garage.

Wallace Gibson, touring manager for Bertram Mills' circus, said that after his return from Belfast, Cullens told him that Musa 'was having a good time in Ireland.' Later he had claimed to have had a letter from Musa who 'was having a good time in London.'

A 'Miss X', chambermaid in a London hotel, said Cullens told her that he and Assim had packed Musa back to Turkey because he 'hit the old man.'

All this, the Crown said, showed Cullens trying to cover his tracks, but they had yet another witness to produce, one who clinched the case beyond doubt. He was James Hagan, a farmer who had lived near Carrickfergus. On the night of 2nd September, the Wednesday on which Cullens and Musa had said goodbye to their lodging-house landlady in Belfast, he was driving along the lane at Seskin. Halfway down the lane the way was blocked by a large car... a cream and brown Essex saloon. Thinking something was wrong, he stopped. The man behind the wheel asked him if he was on the right road for Larne. Mr Hagan gave him directions and then asked if anything was wrong. The man said, 'No I'm alright.'

The man with whom he had this midnight encounter was Eddie Cullens, said Mr Hagan. After this evidence the man in the dock did not have a chance. Hagan's evidence placed him at the scene of the murder on the night it happened. The final piece in the Crown case was placed in the pattern by Robert Churchill, the famous London gunsmith who was a consultant for Scotland Yard. He proved that the bullet which killed Musa came from the 'vestpocket' Walther .25 pistol found in Cullens' lodgings at Liverpool.

Eddie Cullens tried desperately to explain away the damning chain of circumstantial evidence against him. The locked garage in Liverpool, he said, was used by Musa and his 'lady friends.' The Turk, he said, could not leave women alone and had fixed the lock on the inside of the garage so he could take girls there and be undisturbed. The gun, he said, belonged to Musa; the name 'Barney Berman' was used by Musa, not him, because the Turk was 'ashamed of his name.' Cullens also swore that Musa had deserted him in Belfast on the night he and Ryan had gone to Celtic Park. 'Musa would not come inside the dog track,' he told the court, 'he just sat outside sulking and saying he wanted to go back to Derry because he had met a rich girlfriend there.'

When he and Ryan came out of the stadium, Musa had gone. They searched for him in several pubs and then assumed he had gone to Derry by train. He left Belfast alone. Ryan was mistaken in saying Musa was in the car when he left the Donegall Quay lodgings.

As for telling the circus manager that he had letters from Musa,

Cullens explained, this was only a story to cover for Musa. Asked point-blank by his own Council if he had killed the Turk, Cullens raised his right hand and half-rising from the witness-box, said dramatically: 'Before God and man, I swear I did not.'

Assim Redvan, the other syndicate partner, called by the defence, did his best for Cullens. The pick and shovel found under such suspicious circumstances in the 'burial' garage 'had been ordered by him - to dig drains around the tent where the 'Oldest Man in The World' was exhibited.

Mr Lowry also did his best for his client and he had some minor points to score. Peggy Murphy, questioned about the 'bathing-cap' episode, said she thought that something pink had fallen from the towel. The defence produced a pink rubber bag which he said Cullens kept for carrying cash from the sale of Agha's photographs. Then there was the size and weight of the dead Turk. 'Looking at the man in the dock,' Mr Lowry told the jury, 'you're a small attenuated figure of the man who is supposed to have handled this 14 stone six-footer over a two and a half foot stone wall. To throw that body over would have been an impossibility except for Hercules,' said the barrister.

Mr Lowry also pointed to the lack of motive and suggested the theory that Musa, 'a man of exceedingly loose morality where women were concerned,' had got away from Ryan and Cullens at the greyhound track and got into trouble somewhere in Belfast because of his 'inordinate immoralities.' This, he thought, had led to the Turk's death.

But the excuses of the little American and the pleas of his Council were useless. The jury returned a verdict of guilty and the Lord Chief Justice put on the dreaded black cap.

Eddie Cullens was hanged in Belfast Prison at 8 am on 13th January 1932. He was the only Jew ever to be hanged in Ireland and was attended by Rabbi Schachter, Belfast's Jewish leader.

For the rabbi, the last act in the drama was awful. He was advised by his doctors not to attend but insisted he would not leave Cullens to face death alone.

The condemned man was composed to the end and was writing messages to his family in New York up until five minutes before the governor of the prison arrived at the cell to take him to the scaffold. 'For me it was a terrible strain,' said Rabbi Schachter. 'Cullens showed bravery beyond imagination. He had a smiling face when he parted and repeated again and again that he was going to meet his maker with the full satisfaction that his hands were clean of the blood of a murdered man.'

Eddie Cullens' protestations of innocence on the gallows may have been impressive but all the crushing weight of evidence placed him at the right time at the cornfield which still holds some of the secrets of Ulster's strangest murder.

The Execution of Harold Courtney
on 7th April 1933

The foul deed came to light when on the 23rd August 1932 a group of children came across the body of a woman lying in some bushes near Derryane, Co. Armagh. The local police were contacted who in turn set up a murder investigation, the C.I.D. from Belfast were informed and it was they who took over the murder case.

It was not long before the body was identified as of one Minnie Reid. Her throat had been cut. It was Head Constable Slack of the C.I.D. and District Inspector Anderson who conducted the investigation. Their efforts were hampered by the dense undergrowth at the scene of the crime, nevertheless their perseverance and thoroughness were rewarded for a blood stained razor was found in the undergrowth about 14 feet from the body.

It took the C.I.D. a fortnight before an arrest was made. All inquiries led them to a young man by the name of Harold Courtney. He was brought to Coalisland for questioning and it was at the end of these interviews that he was charged with the murder and taken into custody.

Courtney in his statement acknowledged that he had known Minnie Reid for four or five years but that he had not kept her company during that time. He also stated that he had heard that she had gone to Portadown to work and had not known where she was until he read of her death in the papers. It was from the same article in the newspaper he states, that he read that she had gone to Vernersbridge Station and then to Verner's Inn to meet a man on the Monday before her death. When further questioned by the C.I.D. Courtney could not account for his own movements on that date. He claimed that as he was to so many places it was hard to narrow it down to a specific location.

At the early part of the investigation his clothes were taken from him and sent to London for forensic examination.

Courtney was returned for trial at the Ulster Winter Assizes at Downpatrick before Lord Justice Andrews and like all murders of the period it was reported in depth all over the province. His defence claimed he was 'Not Guilty' whilst it sought to prove that the woman had possibly committed suicide. Courtney was defended by Mr Wm. Lowry K.C. and Mr B.J. Fox The trial lasted 5 days with almost fifty witnesses being examined.

It was during the direct examination by the Crown that Courtney admitted that practically all his statements to the police were fabricated, but he stated his reason for this was that he was engaged and he did not want his name linked to Minnie Reid. He went on to state that Minnie Reid had arranged to meet him at Portadown on the 12th July. She told him that she was in trouble (expecting a baby - their baby). He promised to make inquiries regarding her confinement to hospital and arranged to meet her at Vernersbridge to tell her of the results of these inquiries. He stated that he went there but did not see her. He then stated, "I wrote to her asking her to meet me, I even hired out a car to keep our appointment, but on the Tuesday night I decided to have nothing more to do with the whole affair and wrote a letter to her to that effect. The letter, it was claimed, was posted in Aughnacloy.

He was subjected to a thorough cross-examination by the Attorney General, who was the Right Honourable A.B. Babington K.C. on behalf of the Crown. Like most Irish murder cases the jury were always reluctant to pass the motion of guilty as it meant the death sentence. So they disagreed, with the result that Courtney was sent forward to the Armagh Assizes.

It was here that practically the same evidence was presented again, but the defence brought in strengthened evidence that the wound had been suicidal. As before, the trial lasted 5 days but the jury returned the verdict of guilty with their recommendation for mercy. Before passing the death sentence, the Lord Chief Justice (Right Honourable Sir William Moore) said he cordially approved of the verdict, but profoundly disagreed with their recommendation for mercy.

As was the case with most of the other murderers I've covered in this book when the prisoner is faced with the reality of being in front of his maker within minutes, they usually confess their guilt on the gallows platform. The question would have been asked by the hangman, "Have you anything to say before I do my duty?" and at this late stage, knowing hat there would be no reprove, they would have admitted to the offence. On the odd occasion they said nothing. I'm of the opinion that the hangman felt more relieved if he knew he was hanging a guilty person, but the fact remained that Courtney was tried by 12 good men and true, although he protested his innocence to the very end.

It was rumoured at the time, even for years afterwards that Courtney was alive and well in Australia. Similar rumours have circulated about Elvis Presley, the American rock star, claiming that he was alive and well and has been seen in different parts of the world.

I think reporters print this stuff in order to sell their newspapers, but the facts remain according to the death book in H.M.P. Crumlin Road, Belfast.

The City Coroner (Mr T.E. Alexander) held an inquest at the jail at 10am that same morning, just two hours after the execution as was the custom.

Pierrepoint was the executioner, and the witnesses to the execution were, the prison Medical Officer Dr O'Flaherty, Captain R. W. Stevens the prison's Governor and Mr Valentine Wilson the Under-Sheriff for the County of Armagh.

The Medical Officer had attended quite a few hangings in the jail, but Captain Stevens was also present during those early days of hanging but we can see from his title he held the rank of captain. It was the custom in those early days of the penal system to offer posts to ex-military types, as they were used to discipline and most of them would have had a written report given to them on their discharge from the army or the Navy. Even today there are a fair percentage of prison staff who are ex-army, navy or R.A.F. On the same token there are also nurses, teachers and business people who have made the prison service their chosen career.

The odd one out is the Under-Sheriff for the County of Armagh. All the other hangings in H.M.P. Belfast were attended by the Sheriff or Under-Sheriff of Belfast. I think the reasons why he attended was as the hangman's scaffold in Armagh Jail had fallen into disrepair or as the offence happened in County Armagh the Under-Sheriff had to be there to see that justice was carried out according to the law of the court.

In summing up, the Lord Chief Justice states, "I think it was a cold-blooded, calculated and callous murder, and I think you betrayed this girl, and under the stress of her claims upon you, you butchered her and her unborn child."

The Execution of Thomas Joseph Williams
on 2nd September 1942

Thomas Joseph Williams, aged nineteen, of 46 Bombay Street, Belfast, was executed in Belfast Prison for the murder of a police constable on Easter Sunday 1942.

Patrick Murphy was killed in Cawnpore Street after a gang of youths fired on a police patrol from behind an air-raid shelter on Kashmir Road. The constable and his colleagues pursued the gunmen in their van until they sought refuge inside number 53 Cawnpore Street. Constable Murphy was the first to follow them inside, entering by the back door. When his colleagues next saw him, in the scullery, he was dead. Murphy had managed to return fire; he was still clutching his revolver, from which three shots had been fired.

The mystery of the three missing bullets was soon resolved; they were inside Williams, who was admitted to hospital en route to the dock, where he was to face capital charges along with five others, including a woman. They were also sentenced to death, but, unlike Williams, were reprieved.

Shortly before his execution, Williams was visited in prison for the last time by relatives. Among the relatives who came to take their leave of him were his brother Richard, a soldier in the Irish Army Air Corps, his old grandmother, Mr and Mrs C. Fay, his uncle and aunty, with whom he resided, his former employer Mr G. McGowan, printer, and his solicitor, Mr D.P. Mariner. The guests were allowed to stay with Williams for an hour. He embraced them affectionately with tears in his eyes. His brother showed him a telegram from their father, also in the Irish Army, which read, 'Be brave to the end, my son. Goodbye and God bless you.' The prisoner asked his solicitor to convey a message to his friends: 'Thank all for their efforts to save me; I am quite resigned if it is God's holy will and if it is done for Ireland.' Mrs Fay left the prison in a state of collapse and had to be helped into a waiting taxi.

Sentence was carried out on Williams at 8 am and five minutes later a notice was posted on the prison gates:

We, the undersigned, hereby declare that judgment of death was this day executed on Thomas Joseph Williams in His Majesty's Prison of Belfast in our presence, dated the 2nd day of September, signed Robert Henderson, Under-Sheriff of the City of Belfast, Thomas Moore Stewart (Capt), Governor of said prison, Patrick McAllister, Chaplain of said prison.

The interment took place at the prison burial ground at noon. Fathers McAllister, Alexis and McAneaney again officiating. The governor and a number of Roman Catholic warders, according to the Belfast Telegraph, grouped around the grave and stood stiffly to attention as the coffin was lowered into the ground. The entire ceremony lasted only a few minutes.

Pierpont was the executioner and he had an assistant.

The inquest had taken place shortly before, at 11 o'clock, under the auspices of Dr H.P. Lowe, the City Coroner. A jury of fifteen accepted unanimously his invitation to view the body. The only witnesses were Governor Stewart, who gave evidence of identification and of handing the body over to the Under-Sheriff, and the prison doctor, Dr McComb.

Answering the foreman of the jury, the doctor said that the execution had been carried out to the letter of the law and that death had been instantaneous. The jury returned a verdict in accordance with the medical evidence.

Outside, meanwhile, the authorities had taken elaborate precautions to prevent demonstrations, cordoning off a large part of the surrounding area. Police in cars or tenders patrolled the streets, closing off the stretch between Carlisle Circus and Agnes Street, and diverting traffic. Thousands of workers on their way to mills and factories were forced to make a detour. Tramcars were prohibited from stopping inside the sealed-off area. Residents of streets off the Crumlin Road were permitted to pass only on production of their papers.

As 8 am drew nearer, crowds began to gather on the perimeter of the cordon. Here and there a woman would drop to her knees and pray, to be joined by another and yet another, and before long there were scores of them kneeling silently. Many of them had brought along lunch parcels. Tramcars of workers passed. The women began to sing. Most wept. Some carried children in their arms. The crowd soon numbered some two hundred; they were still praying half-an-hour after the execution.

The police intervened at the corner of Old Lodge Road and Florence Place, which runs along the side of the county Court House, when a two-hundred-strong crowd of women and girls launched into

'God Save the King' on the stroke of 8 o'clock. This was immediately afterwards followed with cheers, and then a rendition of 'Land of Hope and Glory' and 'There'll Always Be an England.' On the other side of the street the women carried on praying while the police moved in on the singers and gradually forced them back into a side street.

At another point an altercation typifying the different points of view of the two crowds and ending with the words, 'There are men being killed at the Front every day, and they don't pray for them!' was overheard.'

Some members of the crowd which had been praying around the rim of the exclusion zone at Carlisle Circus drifted off (amid much booing and cheering from the other side) towards the city centre when the police withdrew. They went along one side of Royal Avenue screaming frenziedly and giving Nazi salutes, before making for the Falls Road area, singing Republican songs and waving handkerchiefs and flags. Sweeping along Bombay Street, pausing silently outside Williams' house, they continued their demonstration. When they saw police officers posted at the corner of Mark Street, they dispersed.

Bombay Street itself was quiet throughout the morning of the execution of no. 46's most notorious son. The blinds at that house were drawn and the doors closed. One man who walked in the demonstration said, 'Indignation in the district is very great, we fear trouble.'

In the Nationalist areas of the city, Roman Catholic churches were filled up from 6 am onwards. In some cases, church-goers remained until after requiem mass was celebrated at 8 am.

Further demonstrations were held outside the City Hall where several hundred people, mostly young-girls, assembled and insulted passing American soldiers by giving them Nazi salutes. This mob threatened to get out of hand, but the police handled them with firmness and tact. They were rewarded for their trouble with hails of bottles and other missiles. There were several arrests and, later, prosecutions.

American soldiers were also on the receiving end before the day was out; a U.S. Army car was stoned in Durham Street. The driver was able to accelerate out of danger and no-one in the vehicle was injured.

That afternoon in the Carrick Hill and other Nationalist areas of

Belfast black flags were hoisted on telegraph poles and houses. The police removed them.

Approximately 600 of the 1000 members of the Irish Transport and General Workers' Union employed in Belfast's docklands downed tools when news of the execution broke. Dockers in Newry and Londonderry, and factory girls from that Maiden City, also stopped work briefly.

In Dublin and throughout Éire places of business closed for an hour and flags flew at half-mast. There were large congregations at services in Roman Catholic churches.

The Cloughmills Murder
The Execution of Samuel McLaughlin
on 25th July 1961

Samuel McLaughlin, aged forty, a foundry worker, of Cloughmills, County Antrim was hanged in Belfast Prison on 26th July 1961 for the murder of his wife Nellie (32).

The execution was carried out at 8 am, and, ten minutes later, the customary notice was posted on the prison gates. This was the ninth hanging in Northern Ireland (since August 1922); the previous hanging had been in September 1942.

McLaughlin stood trial for the second time on 25th April for what the Attorney-General described as a brutal killing. His previous appearance had been two months earlier. His address was given as 3 Radstock Gardens, Derby.

The Jury had failed to agree after a five-day hearing at the Winter Assizes in February 1961, and a retrial at the County Antrim Spring Assizes before Mr Justice McVeigh and an all-male jury had been ordered.

McLaughlin pleaded not guilty when arraigned on the charge. In his opening address for the prosecution, the Attorney-General (McGinnes) said Mrs McLaughlin had been brutally attacked, and suggested that the jury would be left in no doubt as to her husband's guilt once they had heard the full story.

McLaughlin, said the Attorney General, had gone home with his wife on the night before her murder (18th October) and, at some time before 7 am the next morning, murdered her.

The victim had been discovered lying on her bed in her two-roomed cottage at Lisban by a policeman that morning. She had head and facial wounds, and a nylon stocking had been tied around her neck.

McGinnes went on to describe how the McLaughlins had been married for ten years. They had no children. Mrs McLaughlin was a native of County Antrim. In 1959 she had returned form Derby, in the English Midlands, where her husband had been working, and settled near Cloughmills. She had begun maintenance proceedings against the accused, and, at Killagan, on 14th October of the previous year, he had been ordered to pay his wife £3 a week. At the end of the hearing McLaughlin had made some remark to the effect that the court need not worry about the details of the maintenance order as the money would not be paid. He had no intention of working hard only to hand over his earnings to his wife. He gave the impression of intending to commit suicide. He had, he said, had a happy stay in England with his wife, but had heard she had been seeing other men.

McGinnes then told the court how the couple had met for the first time since the maintenance order on 17th October. They had drunk together, and McLaughlin had asked his wife to come back to Derby with him. His wife then invited him back to her new house, which she shared with her mother, and he agreed, bringing a carry-out of stout, whiskey and rum. Next day all three lunched together. Later the McLaughlins went out on a motorcycle and paid a number of calls. Mrs McLaughlin's mother, meanwhile, had made arrangements to spend the night elsewhere, so that the couple could have the house to themselves. McLaughlin and his wife were last seen together at 10 pm that night, 18th October.

McLaughlin carried on riding around the district on his bike, calling in on people he knew. At one house the accused told the occupant that he would not be paying any more money to his wife as he had murdered her. He had strangled her, and did not intend to make his escape as he had enough of life. He intended to crash his bike into a church wall.

Later, at another house, McLaughlin allegedly said, 'I strangled her this morning.' He assumed 'they' (the police) were already on his track, and intended to hang himself.

Shortly after 5pm on 19th October a policeman forced a window at the house in order to gain admission. Inside he discovered the woman's partially-clothed body.

The State Pathologist examined the body later that night, at 10.30 pm, and found extensive wounds on the forehead and face, as well as a tightly-tied nylon stocking around the neck. The skull was also fractured. Death, the pathologist concluded, was due to strangulation, accelerated by blows to the head. The blows to the head had been delivered with considerable force while Mrs McLaughlin was still alive. The nature of the marks showed that she had moved her head from side to side as the blows rained down on her. It was not possible to say what weapon(s) had been used, but there were broken pieces of broom handle in the room.

During questioning by the R.U.C., continued McGinnes, McLaughlin had allegedly said, 'I most probably have done it. I'm not certain about what happened. Maybe between nine and ten today, if I tied that stocking around her neck. I may or may not have done it, I just don't know.'

Samuel L. Clare, a Ballymena solicitor, who represented the National assistance Board at the maintenance case at Killagan, told the court that McLaughlin, conducting his own case with some ability, alleged that his wife had been unsettled in Derby and had come back to Northern Ireland on several occasions. She had allegedly been what might be described as nagging and difficult. McLaughlin however, had not made any substantial allegations against her.

As the magistrate considered the date for the payment of the first payment under the maintenance ordered, McLaughlin had, Clare testified, said that he need not bother about the details as the money would never be paid.

Cross-examined by Mr Ambrose McGonigle K.C., Senior Defence Counsel, the witness said that he could not remember the accused asking his wife to come back to him, although he probably said something to that effect and there was mention of a house in Derby.

Mrs Mary Christie of Ballyweaney, sister of the accused, told how her brother was always bright and cheerful; she had never heard him make any threats towards anyone, and seemed very fond of his wife. After the court case, she said when cross-examined, he had begun to drink more than ever before. She had never known him to be objectionable or aggressive when drunk. When he told her on 18th October that he had been with his wife in Cloughmills and that he was to meet her again that evening, she continued, he seemed happy.

Miss Jeanne Mary Christie of Ballyweaney, a farmer, said that McLaughlin had worked for her before and after serving in the R.A.F. When he visited her at 2.25am on 15th October he told her he had lost the maintenance case but was not prepared to fritter away his hard-earned money on his wife. He said he had reached the end of the road and wanted to die. He asked her if she had heard any reports of his wife seeing other men, and she replied that she had not. McLaughlin, she said, looked tired out; he was very much changed since the last time she had seen him in July 1959.

Cross-examined, Miss Christie said she had not known McLaughlin to be bad-tempered or unpleasant, and she never knew him to make threats towards his wife. When she suggested to him that he made

up with her and make a new start, he replied, 'Yes, I still love her.'
A crowd of about 100 had gathered outside the prison on the
Crumlin Road, Belfast. They were mostly men. Some were very
young. One woman, crying into her handkerchief, cried out: 'God
help his poor wife, but it's a pity they have to hang him. He looked
such a quiet fellow.'

Mr Denis Barrit, a member of the Society of Friends, made a personal
protest. In fifty years' time, he argued, this event would be looked
back upon with the same attitude that people now had towards
hunting. Hanging was a terrible, uncivilised thing.

The jostling crowd had to be held back by police when a warder in
blue overalls and Mr R. Frazer, Prison Clerk of Works, appeared to
post the notice stating that McLaughlin had been executed.

McLaughlin's appeal to the Court of Criminal Appeal, claiming that
he was a delirious alcoholic, failed. So did two petitions - one signed
by 700 former neighbours in Derby, the other by 150 Cloughmills
people. The Governor, Lord Wakehurst, acting on the advice of the
cabinet, had decided that the law must take its course.

The hangman was Mr Harry Allen. He was assisted by Mr J.
Richard. The two men left the prison two hours after the hanging
and returned to England.

The Execution of Robert McGladdery
on 20th December 1961

A neighbour exercising his greyhounds on the Damolly Road in Newry on the morning of 28th January 1961 came across a black shoe lying by the side of the road not far from the Gamble's home. A little further on he noticed a black silk scarf in a ditch by the Damolly Crossroads and more footwear: a pair of brown shoes and another black one. Further ahead, on the old Belfast Road, he saw a bicycle. Robert McClouchenraner, a farm labourer, was busy fitting a new gate across the entrance to a field. The two men chatted, not attaching a great deal of importance to the articles of footwear and clothing scattered roundabout. The greyhound fancier went on his way with his dogs and the labourer mounted his bike and cycled to Primrose Hill he could not find the sledge he had left there the night before. Curious, he cycled back and had another closer look at the clothing. There was blood on the scarf. He hurried over to the Gambles'.

Mrs Gamble and one of her daughters returned to the spot with him. The mother picked up the clothing and shoes. Her daughter found a handbag in the field by the roadside. The last time they had seen these things had been the evening before when their daughter and elder sister, Pearl had been putting them on to go to a local dance. A million thoughts raced through their minds. Where was Pearl? What had happened to her?

McClouchenraner dashed up the road to the Copeland's and phoned for the police, before returning to the Gambles. Then things began to take a dramatic turn. Constable Bamford received McClouchenraner's call and reported it, in turn, to Head Constable Orr. Another head constable, O'Hare, was dispatched to the Gamble's house, which was situated some 240 yards from the crossroads. Mrs Gamble showed him the Articles of clothing they had found. By this stage, as was pointed out at the trial, a blood-stained overcoat, a light grey skirt, a pair of panties, a black belt, a brush and a comb had also been discovered nearby. McClouchenraner informed the policeman of some traces of earthen disturbances on a bank near the gap into the field about 170 yards from the crossroads. Immediately the policeman began to organise a search of the area. A button and a blood-stained handkerchief were found in this field, Weir's Field, about thirty yards from the gap.

Close on 100 police and civilians took part in the day-long search which took them over a bog and a field. Pearl Gamble's body was eventually located about a mile away. The search became one of the most concentrated murder-hunts ever launched in Northern Ireland.

Heartbroken and red-eyed, Mrs Gamble and her husband, Robert, a pensioner, were informed of the sad find. The Gamble family consisted of these two and their children; four other girls and a boy. They lived in a farm cottage. On the evening of 27th January 1961, Pearl Gamble, an outfitter's buyer, aged nineteen, was dropped off home by her two companions at her home at Primrose Hill, just over two miles from Newry at Damolly. They called back for her later that evening and all three set off for a dance organised by the local Rangers and Girl Guides troop at the Henry Thompson Memorial Orange Hall on the Downshire Road in Newry.

Mrs Gamble later testified that she had left the key in the front door so that when Pearl came home she could let herself in without disturbing the rest of the household.

At 5am Mrs Gamble got up to make breakfast for her son and another daughter who left home at 6 o'clock to start work in a Newry factory. She had noticed Pearl's absence, but was not unduly worried, assuming that her daughter had stayed over at a friend's house. Although the other members of the family were concerned, it was not until McClouchenraner knocked on the door at 9am that she started to worry.

Pearl's body, found in a lump of whins, and in such a position as to suggest that it had been dropped from some height, had, testified Inspector Bradley, been naked except for a pair of stockings. A white blouse, underskirt and bra had been found by the body, which was found lying face downwards. The face was stained with blood, the lips swollen, and there was an inch-long cut above and close to the right eyebrow. The bridge of the nose was bruised and discoloured, as were both eyes. The throat was also bruised and marked near the windpipe. There were several stab wounds on the front of the body; one was about four inches above the left breast, another between the breastbone and the nipple. The remainder of the District Inspector's findings were banned from publication. Sergeant McKeown of the R.U.C.'s photographic department had taken photos of the area where the body had been found.

Pearl's body had been removed to Belfast the day after its discovery at the request of the State Pathologist, W. Campbell. Dr D.K. Marshall performed the post mortem. The body was then removed to Banbridge, where Dr B. Orr, coroner, opened an inquest which was adjourned after formal identification.

Next to give evidence was one of Pearl's friends. She identified the pair of brown shoes as Pearl's. She then went on to describe how she had gone out to join Billy Martin and Derek Shanks in the car, while Pearl had gone with Joe Clidesdale. They had waited for her in the car for ten or fifteen minutes. She then got into the car and they drove to Damolly crossroads, near Cross House. They started to turn right, but Pearl insisted on getting out. She was wearing the black shoes and carrying the brown ones. The car then moved off; Pearl's friend never saw her alive again.

This had happened around 2.30am - the dance had ended half-an-hour before.

Miss A. Boyd, an 18-year-old shop assistant, of Cribe Road, Newry told the court how she had seen Pearl dancing with a young man by the name of McGladdery at least twice between 1.15 and 1.30am. She had herself danced with him before Pearl. He had been wearing a light blue suit, something about his neck, and black shoes. She had not then seen any marks on McGladdery's face. She had last seen her friend dash across the road towards her own lane.

The District Inspector stated that he had interviewed McGladdery at the police station in connection with the murder of Pearl Gamble. He had pointed out the fur-collared short overcoat, tie, handkerchief, and a pair of gent's black shoes found by the police. Had McGladdery wanted to say anything? He had nothing to say.

Robert A. McGladdery, whose address was given as Damolly village, Newry, a short distance from where Pearl had lived at Upper Damolly, was twenty-six years old. By occupation he was a labourer. He was accused of the murder of Pearl Gamble on 11th April 1961.

At the trial, at Newry Murder Court, Clause 42 was invoked; this means that particulars of a considerable part of the evidence were prohibited. McGladdery wore a black suit and an open scarlet shirt at his trial; he carried a number of sheets of paper and a pencil, and seemed to make notes during the trial. He smiled occasionally.

Mrs Gamble wept as her daughter's clothing was displayed as evidence.

McGladdery was found guilty, sentenced to death, and executed at H.M.P. Belfast on the 20th December 1961. The hangman was Harry Allen, who departed (back to England) almost immediately after the execution with his assistant. Chaplain T. Vance attended to McGladdery prior to his execution.

McGladdery had, at the end of his trial in October at Downpatrick Assizes, protested his innocence. His appeal, however, was dismissed in the Court of Criminal Appeal after a four-day hearing, and he was refused leave to appeal to the House of Lords. His last hope gone, he asked for his admission of guilt to be made known.

The Murder At The Bank
The Execution of Sub-Inspector Montgomery in Omagh Jail, August 1873

118 years on, the murder at the bank is still a talking point in Newtownstewart. There are stories of the ghost of William Glass haunting the building, which still stands, much as it was then, in the main street of the County Down town.

There is also the story of the 'Missing Witness', a local man who emigrated to America just after the murder and later returned, some years after Montgomery was hanged. He told friends that he had looked through the window of the bank to check the time on the clock at 3pm on the day of the murder and saw Montgomery standing at the counter. When news of the murder broke, a few hours later, he had already packed his bags and was on his way to catch the train to Londonderry, where he was to sail for the Untied States. Realising if he gave information, he would be held as a material witness, and miss his sailing, he decided to say nothing.

All night the thunder rumbled over Omagh. Folk huddled in their houses and listened to the rain pelting against the window and drumming on their rooftops, blinking at the flashes of lightening and waiting for the roar of thunder to follow in its wake.

At 7.45am the bell of the County Jail began to toll, struggling to make itself heard above the sound of the storm. A quarter of an hour later the bell ceased to toll just as the last peel of thunder died away. The rain stopped too, and the wind dropped to a breeze.

On the flagpole above the prison walls the black flag fluttered and the bell began to peel dismally.

The date was 26th August 1873. It was a time when people still believed in signs from Heaven, and that morning they interpreted the storm as a sign of the Almighty's wrath, regarding the thunder which stopped at precisely 8am as the last flamboyant act in a drama which had been 'the country's talk' for more than two years.

Inside the jail, at precisely 8am, Thomas Hartley Montgomery was hanged and the file was closed on one of the strangest murder cases that Ulster has ever seen.

The Newtownstewart murder is more mysterious, more quirky, than many a thriller. People throughout Northern Ireland talked of little else. The sensational aspects of the case drew Fleet Street's attention - a rare event in those days of mail-boats and 'special telegrams.' Scotland Yard even sent over a detective to assist the R.I.C., the Royal Irish Constabulary.

Not only was the murder particularly gory - the medical evidence made jurors pale - but its central characters and location were so respectable that the public was both shocked and revolted.

Let us begin at the very beginning ... on a sunny day in the quiet town of Newtownstewart on 29th June 1871. It was a day like any other. By early afternoon the main street was deserted but for a couple of old ladies in shawls peering into the windows of McDowell's General Store and two lads playing on the pavement outside the bank. And then there was Patrick Nocher, a tired, hungry, out-of-work labourer, dozing on the steps of a lodging-house.

Into view comes a donkey-cart and two men, fishermen from Donegall selling cockles. From an upstairs window of the bank they are heard by Fanny McBride, housemistress of the bank manager, M Strahan. She recognises the men from a previous visit and decides that her master would be pleased with a dinner of cockles after returning from his busy day at the fair at Drumquin. Below, in the office, is 22-year-old William Glass, in sole charge of the day's takings of £1,600. Conscientiously, aware of the responsibility placed upon him, he is checking the sovereigns and notes before locking them away in the safe. With him is the man who plans to kill him.

Fanny, carrying a pail, leaves the bank by the front door, leaving it ajar, crosses the street to the fishermen, and begins to haggle over the cockles. A small crowd has gathered around the Donegall men; laughter and banter breaks the sultry silence of the June day.

The two boys interrupt their play to look on and, in a lull, hear a strange noise from within the bank. Later they say it sounded like heavy footsteps, moaning and a 'squeal.'

It is 3pm and inside the bank William Glass lies dead. His murderer crams packets of bank notes into his pockets.

At 4.15pm Fanny, having cleaned and prepared the cockles for the evening meal, goes to check the time. The nearest clock is the one in the bank's main office. She peers through the glass door and gives a scream. On the floor she sees William Glass's dead body sprawled in a pool of blood.

For an hour Newtownstewart knows something is terribly wrong at the bank. But what? Fanny rushes to McDowell's shop and tells the owner that William must be sick. These were, after all the days when T.B. ended in a massive haemorrhage.

McDowell sees Glass, and the gore, and assumes that the young man has cut his throat. No-one thinks of murder; this is Newtownstewart, after all.

But William Glass had been killed by 12 blows, from a bill-hook, to the head. Three of the blows had split his skull. A spike, forced through his ear, was a final, and unnecessary, coup de grace.

When the police - first the Duty Constable from the barracks and then, an hour later, the Sub-Inspector (the equivalent of today's rank of District Inspector) - arrived, they examined the body and decided to call in senior officers from Omagh and Londonderry. A local bigwig, Commander Scott J.P., ex-RN (retired), also arrives at the blood-splashed bank and assumes command, ordering the Sub-Inspector to send a telegram to Dublin Castle, H.Q. of the R.I.C. He suggests that the wording of the telegram be altered, from 'suspicious circumstances' to 'brutal murder.' The Sub-Inspector remains silent, but changes the wording to 'supposed murder' and signs his name on the telegram: Thomas Hartley Montgomery, adding his rank.

The next day Ulster read of the 'horrible and brutal murder at Newtownstewart.' All the lurid details were described in rolling Victorian sentences: blood, savagery, horror, and all in sleepy little Newtownstewart. The 'murderous attack' said the News-Letter, had begun in the bank's inner office; marks on the doorposts showed that the 'assassin' had followed his victim, aiming blows, to fell him finally in the outer office. The sum of £1,605 was missing, and directors of the Northern Bank offered a reward of £100 for evidence leading to the conviction of the murderer ... or £50 for evidence securing an arrest.

But it was not until the inquest two days later that the biggest sensation of the murder occurred. From witnesses in the street that fatal, sunny afternoon, came evidence pointing unerringly at one man - Sub-Inspector Montgomery!

Nocher, the tramp, said he had seen Montgomery enter the bank at 11.15 and leave at 3.30. Mary Ann Cameron said she had looked out of McDowell's shop and seen a young man peering around the front door of the bank. She described him as a 'dark eyed, good-looking man with dark whiskers and a black beard.' Asked if she could identify him in the Coroner's Court, she pointed to Montgomery.

Three other witnesses identified Montgomery as the man who left the bank and walked briskly down a side-street, a coat over his arm, half an hour after the murder.

The most damning evidence of all came from Miss Mary Thompson, a visitor who was staying with the Strahans at the bank-house. She said that Montgomery had come into the living-room of the house between 2pm and 3pm and asked when the manager would be back from the Drumquin fair. 'He said he wanted to see Mr Strahan about going fishing,' she said.

But Mr Strahan himself testified that he never went fishing with the Sub-Inspector. In fact, he didn't even know that the man was interested in fishing at all.

Montgomery left the inquest with the verdict of the jury ringing in his ears: 'wilful murder by Thomas Hartley Montgomery.' Outside, a crowd had grown. Women hissed, men booed. The constables protecting him from the mob were still, technically at least, under his command, but they had orders from the County Inspector to keep Montgomery under house arrest. For weeks Montgomery lived in the barracks, doing routine work; he even signed the weekly bank order for the station's wages. But public feeling against him was running so high that the authorities decided it would be safer to take him to Omagh Prison to await arraignment. The townspeople of Newtownstewart had liked Glass and known that the policeman was his friend. The suspicion that Montgomery had murdered Glass outraged them. That the man charged with the murder had been charged with preventing such events horrified them even more. For two years the Newtownstewart murder was big news. At the Assizes on 1st March 1872 the case was postponed. Over the next 18 months there were three long trials at the first two the jurors disagreed. A witness gave evidence of Montgomery leaving the bank furtively, of seeing him on the afternoon of the murder in a field where, later, the missing money was discovered. Strahan recalled how Montgomery frequented the bank daily and commented on how easy it would be to murder the cashier and make off with the takings. Defence experts said that there had been no blood on Montgomery's clothing, but police doctors explained how the first blow with the billhook (found in the same field with the money) would have stopped glass's heart and prevented any spurts of blood. Montgomery himself did not give evidence; his defence was that he had entered the bank by the front door, left ajar by Fanny

McBride, and gone straight upstairs to speak to Mrs Thompson. He had left minutes later. At the third trial, the motive for the murders was revealed. Montgomery had been speculating unwisely on the Stock Exchange and was now heavily in debt. Not only had he lost £800 inherited from his father, he had also blown £300 belonging to wife, as well as smaller amounts given to him for investment by police colleagues.

A letter to his uncle, Rev. Joseph Bradshaw, pleading for money to settle his accounts was read in court, and the prosecution made great play of the fact that days before the murder Montgomery had received a final demand from the bank.

The jury, this time, took only twenty minutes to return a verdict of guilty. The judge asked Montgomery if he had anything to say before sentence was passed, and it was at this point that the whole case took its most sensational turn.

As those thronging the public gallery leaned forward, Montgomery - pale but composed - made a statement that brought gasps of astonishment:

'I wish to say, m'lord, that at the time of the perpetration of the murder, and for 12 months before that, I was in a state of complete insanity. In the month of June, 1870, I was invited to the residence of Mr. Bradshaw. At the time I was in excellent health. I was there deliberately drugged and poisoned with the object of making me weak-minded.'

The stir this caused in the crowded courtroom had to be quelled by the judge and ushers calling for silence. Montgomery then went on to say that, feeling ill, he had gone to a doctor, who had told him that he had but a few days to live. "He said, 'You may be dead in a week, you can scarcely recover,' and in that state I was compelled to, or at least directed to, marry, and, being weak minded, I consented."

Until this moment there had been a swing of sympathy towards Montgomery in the country, particularly among the ladies who thronged the court each day. But, in his extraordinary statement, he had libelled not only the uncle who had helped him financially, but the wife who had stuck by him throughout the whole long business. As the horrified spectators watched, Montgomery went on to describe how, after marriage, his health and 'weak-mindedness' had worsened, and how he had speculated foolishly and lost vast sums:

'It was at this time that the monomania of attacking banks took possession of me and I said repeatedly to several persons and members of the Constabulary how this sort of thing could be perpetrated and that I myself would do it.'

He described how when stationed in Newtownards, he had told an orderly that he would kill a cashier at the bank in Holywood and carry the money to the top of Cave-Hill where he would live in a 'sod house.' 'Of course the man said I was mad and followed me all that day,' he said.

By the time he had transferred to Newtownstewart, he was in a state of 'derangement and complete lunacy,' sleeping at night with towels round his head to relieve his pains.

The sensational statement from the dock ended:

'One of the Aborigines of New Zealand could scarcely have done anything worse. I was demented, being at the time deficient of reason, and there is a great difference between my case and that of a man who knowingly and wilfully commits an act of the kind. In my case, I was in an entirely helpless state, weak-minded and silly. I don't think a man in that state of mind should have visited on him an act of a man in the possession of his senses.'

Uproar broke out as Montgomery sat down. After two years of legal fights and forthright denials of guilt, he had confessed, pleading insanity. The judge, of course, ruled the plea inadmissible and donned the black cap to condemn the ex-Sub-Inspector to death. The sentence made headlines all over the British Isles. It was the most sensational murder for years and the press wanted every detail. So persistent were the reporters that they were even granted an interview with Montgomery in the condemned cell! Lying on his cot, he greeted them civilly and filled in some missing links in the case. Saying that the murder now seemed like a dream to him, Montgomery described how he had carried the money from the bank in the pinned-up sleeves of his overcoat. He had admitted to having been in the inner office of the bank chatting to Glass for most of the morning. When the last customer had left and the doors were closed, he had produced the billhook blade from his pocket, thrown it on the table in front of the cashier and told him, to take care for he had before him a dangerous man. Glass had laughed at the man he mistook for a friend. As the reporters scribbled notes, Montgomery continued with his macabre press conference:

'I almost killed him with the first blow. He then turned round and looked at me pitifully, then staggered to the door (to the outer office). I gave him the other blows when he was lying on the floor quite dead.' Asked why he had thought it necessary to push the spike through Glass's ear, Montgomery replied:

'I don't know. I sat down on a chair to read the paper while he was moaning and, when he was dead, I knelt down beside him and hacked his head.'

It is clear from this grisly narrative that Montgomery was either trying to reinforce his claim to be mad or was, in fact, really insane. In 1873 executions were events in which the public took a morbid interest. By custom, the press were allowed to witness 'the sacrifice demanded by the law' and comment freely on the skill or otherwise of the hangman, the condemned man's demeanour, and other little gossipy items. On the morning of Montgomery's execution, however, they wrote furiously about this curtailment of their freedom. They went as far as saying that the public could not be quite sure that Montgomery had been hanged, and started a rumour that powerful friends had rigged the execution and allowed Montgomery to escape. But Montgomery did hang---and the thunder which terrified the God-fearing people of Omagh ceased.

Armour's Hole
The Execution of Edward Armour
at Downpatrick Gaol

On the steep, rocky shores of the county Down coastline, near the seaside resort of Newcastle, there is an awesome cleft, through whose narrow vertical walls the Irish Sea had been surging backwards and forwards long, long before the events described in this sorry tale. It is a frightening place, from whose grassy lip the chasm plunges eighty feet to the sea-smoothed rocks below, and visitors stand well back from the edge to peer cautiously into its depths, for the cleft has already claimed at least one victim, from whom it takes its name: Armour's Hole. Perhaps the visitors' caution is excessive. Thomas Armour did not fall to his death on the rocks below after losing his balance while gazing over the precipce and admiring the scenery; he was given a helping-hand by his own son on one of Ulster's most shocking murders. Now, Armour Snr was a well-to-do farmer from Ballaghannery, which nestles, like Newcastle itself, in the Mountains of Mourne. He farmed the best land in the neightbourhod and lived frugally with his son, Edward. Thomas prospered and enjoyed a quiet life. He prided himself on his fields of fat cattle and in his well-stocked barns. The only blot on his landscape was his ne'er-do-well son.

Weary of his father's simple lifestyle and cautiousness when it came to money, young Edward spent most of his time boozing with a wild gang of local rakes. A giant of a man, with immense strengh, anyone who picked a fight with Eddie lived to rue the day; he could fell a man with a single punch. Eddie, though, was no match for his cronies at the card table. He tried his luck night after night and, more often than not, lost heavily. Unfortuntely, the more he lost the more determined he became to play on in an attempt to recoup his losses. Before long he had exhausted his allowance and approached his father to demand more. The old man gave in with reluctance, throwing in a lecture on his son's wild life into the bargain. When, oh when, was he ever going to settle down and marry? Edward promised that it would be soon and then went back to the card table. And so it went on, for more than a year: the son squandered the father's hard-earned money; the father lectured the son, and so on. Eventually things came to a head with Thomas saying enough was enough, no more money for gambling. There was a violent argument, but the old man remained adamant and Edward stormed off angrily. Eddie couldn't bear the idea of giving up gambling. For days on end, he moped around the farm, sullen and barely giving his father the time of day, but all the while his brain was ticking over, hatching a dreadful plan. After a week Edward Armour decided the time had come to put into motion the frist part of that plan. Seemingly contrite, he went to his father and asked the old man's forgiveness for surliness. 'I'm going to turn over a new leaf, 'he lied. 'I think I'll take your advice and settle down.' Thomas was a happy man indeed, especially when his son told him of his intention to marry as soon as possible. Did Eddie have a girl in mind? Eddie just smiled. He had indeed, and she was one of the prettiest girls in the whole of the County of Down; Rose O'Hagan. He told his father how he had first clapped eyes on her some months before at the fair at Hilltown and had been courting her ever since. And not only had she beauty going for her; her father owned a large farm and she would come complete with a handsome dowry. Edward suggested eagerly that he and his father visit the O'Hagans the very next day to fix a wedding date. So next morning Thomas and his seemingly reformed son saddled their horses and set out for the O'Hagan family to visit their future in-laws. But, little did Thomas know, it was a wedding destined never to take place. Indeed, they would never even make it to the O'Hagans, for as they rode along the coast and arrived at a bridge, the calm of the morning was suddenly shattered. Edward turned sullen all of a sudden and picked a quarrel with his father, whom he accused of being a miser. He bellowed at the old man who protested and remined Edward of his earlier promises to change for the better. The son answered by grabbing the father by the coat and pulling him off his horse. A struggle on the muddy track ensued; Thomas tried desperately to ward off the blows Edward rained down on him but was caught by them and ended up, stunned, on his back. When he came to Thomas felt himself being dragged across a field. Above Edward's laboured breathing he could make out the sound of the sea and realised that it was getting closer and closer: Edward was trailing him towards it. Horrified, Thomas tried to break free; they were now but a few yards from the cliff. At the very edge, Thomas resorted to pleading with his son, offering him all he had if he would only let him go. But it was all no avail; Edward turned a deaf ear to his father's pleas and tried to heave him over the edge. In sheer terror, the father made one last almighty effort, fought back, tore at his son's clothing, gripped him around around the knees. But Thomas was merely delaying the inevitable. After a few more minutes the younger man's strengh prevailed and Thomas was hurled screaming over the cliff and dashed on the rocks below before ending up in the sea itself. Thomas's last scream had alerted some fishermen lifting nets near the mouth of the Cleft. They made for the thundering cavern and retrieved Thomas's battered body. In his still clenched fist they found a scrap of cloth ripped from his son's coat. Later, when the Armour farm was found deserted, the search for Edward began. He was found within a day, drinking in a public house some 20 miles from the crime and trying to sell his father's horse. When the arresting-party arrived, Edward attempted to bolt through a window, but was stopped, and, after offering fierce resistance to his would-be-captors, bound with rope. Armour's insane temper and his enormous strengh gave his jailers in the county jail at Downpatrick headache after headache. The strongest irons in the prison proved useless for restraining him; he snapped them as if they were daisy-chains. A blacksmith was sent for and a pair of manacles forged. These were displayed, until a few years ago, at the old prison as 'Armour's bolts.' At his trial Edward Armour sullenly denied all knowledge of his father's murder but the evidence against him was overwhelming. While awaiting the death penalty, Armour became increasingly violent; jailers were terrified to go near him and his shouts could be heard all over the prison. Then he had a visitor, none other than Rose O'Hagan, the girl he had promised to marry. Rose had aged terribly since the murder; her eyes were black-rimmed from grief, her whole face a living reproach. The jailers had warned her not to go near the maniac in the codemned cell but she would not be dissuaded from seeing Armour. The effect of her appearence on him was dramtic. He stopped ranting and gaped at her in disbelief. When she said his name, he buried his face in his hands and wept. From that day on, until the morning he climbed on the scaffold outside Downpatrick Jail, Edward Armour remained quiet, speaking to no-one. Poor Rose died barely a month later after wandering the countryside, insane with grief. The ghost of Thomas Armour is said to haunt the terrible gully in which he met in his death. Local people claim to have heard at night the sound of a scream and a loud splash.

The Newtownards Beetle Murder of 1905

In the darkest days of World War I when men were dying by the thousand every day, the people of Ulster were shocked suddenly by the death of one young man. He was killed not in the muddy trenches of France but in his own driveway in Newtownards. His name was Willie Quinn, the victim of the notorious 'Beetle Murder' of 1915.

Quinn was battered and left for dead but lived long enough to tell the police of the assault. Standing by his bedside was Samuel Heron, his step-father, the man who was to be arrested at Quinn's funeral and who was later to stand trial, three times for his murder.

The case produced one of the strangest murder weapons ever brought to court and climaxed in what the defence counsel called, 'the most incredible story ever told in a witness-box.' It had been a quiet stag night; a night out with the boys, which for Willie Quinn meant a bit of crack in the Masonic Hall and a couple of jars in a nearby pub. He was in high spirits as he strode home in the winter moonlight, well pleased with his last Saturday night as a bachelor. After all, once he was married on Thursday, there would be few Saturday nights like it; on 20 shillings a week he could ill afford a wife and a social life.

But Willie Quinn would never keep his appointment at the altar; little did he know, but the very steps carrying him through the empty streets of Ards were not taking him home ... they were leading him to his death. The happy young bridegroom-to-be would never have another Saturday night out with the boys ... or for that matter, any other. Instead, his violent death was to trigger off one of Ulster's strangest murder cases, a case in which an accusing finger would be pointed at his own step-father, one of Ards' leading citizens. It was a case featuring one of the oddest murder weapons ever entered as an exhibit in a court of law.

A quarter of an hour after leaving Wallace's Pub, Willie Quinn reached the gate of his home, Flush Hall. It was a few minutes after midnight. Willie opened the white-painted wrought iron gates and slammed them shut behind him. As it was dark in the shade of the trees, he moved cautiously towards the house. Halfway up the drive he heard the gravel crunch and span round. The man was no more than a yard away; he raised his arm and Willie ducked instinctively.

As he did so, he felt something swish past his face. Frightened, Quinn backed away. The man moved too, swinging his arm at the retreating Quinn, who cried out in pain as a blow landed on him and split the skin above his left eye. Stumbling now, Quinn took another blow, this time to the skull, and then another. He slumped down onto the gravel and passed out.

Some five hours later the mistress of Flush Hall was roused from her sleep by a noise. Lying in the darkness, she strained to hear above her husband's heavy snoring. There it was again: a barely audible whimper and a tapping on the front door. Grabbing a lamp, she crept downstairs and opened the door slowly, recoiling in horror at what she saw. There, sprawled on the doorstep, was a man moaning softly. When he lifted his head to her, Mrs Samuel Heron recognised the bloody dirtied face of her step-son, Willie Quinn.

The household was roused. Her other step-son, Samuel jnr., rushed downstairs and brought Quinn in, laying him down on the sofa. Rubbing the sleep from his eyes, her husband focussed on the lad's injuries. 'My God,' he cried, 'Willie has got a terrible battering.' Willie was carried into the bedroom where Mrs Heron washed the blood and muck from his face. The gash above his eye measured about two inches but was no longer bleeding. The eye itself was black and swollen. 'Maybe he's not too bad after all,' ventured Samuel Heron.

His wife shot him a glance, motioned to the crimson stain spreading slowly on the pillow on which Willie's head rested. 'He's still losing blood; you'd better send for the doctor.' She gently lifted Willie's head from the pillow and turned it to the side. At the back of the skull were a further two wounds, one oozing blood. It seemed an artery had been severed.

Dr. Jamison sighed resignedly when his telephone rang at 5.45 on Sunday morning; patients, he mused, never stop to think that the doctor might not be feeling too well himself. He decided that if it were something unimportant he would fob the caller off with some excuse or other about being down with the flu and unable to come out. But as soon as he lifted the receiver, he knew he simply had to go, for it was none other than Samuel Heron, one of the most important patients, and a very agitated Samuel Heron at that.

After flinging on some clothes, the doctor drove over to Flush Hall, the big house which Heron occupied as manager of the Ulster Print Works. Waiting at the front door, the doctor noticed the blood on the steps and realised that Heron's anxiety was well grounded. Once inside, he was thanked by Heron for coming so quickly and was taken to Quinn. Willie was still unconscious and Mrs Heron was busily attempting to stem the flow of blood from his battered head. She made way as the doctor entered the bedroom. 'Thank God you're here, doctor; Willie's in a bad way. He's lost a lot of blood.' The doctor cleaned and dressed young Quinn's wounds with skill. As he worked, Mrs Heron filled him in on the details, telling him how she found her step-son lying by the front door. Anxiety seemed to fill the bedroom. Willie had turned as pale as the bandages wrapped around his head. His blackened eye was swollen shut and his breathing was shallow.

'Will he be alright?' asked Samuel Heron It was a question which, in the coming weeks, would assume a sinister air. The step-father's concern, it was whispered, was not for Willie, but reserved for himself, for, even as Heron had asked the question, Willie had stirred and regained consciousness.

That the victim lived long enough to tell the tale of how he was attacked is not the strangest aspect of the Ard's murder; stranger still was the presence at the bedside of the man who, two days later was charged with his murder.

Now Samuel Heron was a man of considerable standing in the County Down market town. As manager of the local mill, he lived well and enjoyed the power he had, in those lean days of 1915, to hire and fire. Heron was married for the third time. His first wife had died at the turn of the century after producing his eldest son, Samuel jnr. A year later he married the widowed Mrs. Quinn, a Newry woman, bringing her and her son, Willie to Flush Hall. Mrs Quinn died in 1908 and, not long after, Heron married again. The last marriage had given him three children.

Flush Hall ranked among the finest houses in the whole of Newtownards. It even came with a servants' cottage. Heron, though, did not actually own it; it was a 'perk.' This did not diminish the pride he felt at living there; he was a man who set much store by appearance. It goes without saying that the upkeep of Flush Hall cost him dear, but then Heron enjoyed the conspicuous consumption that went with life there. Lately, though, he had been feeling the pinch. His salary had amounted to £300 per annum, a sizable income in those days, but the War was at its height and, as a result, business at the printworks had slumped. The directors had forced him to accept a cut of £200 per year.

His declining fortunes, coupled with some substantial debts he had incurred, was to be a plank in the prosecution's case against Samuel Heron.

All Sunday Willie Quinn slipped into and out of consciousness. It was not until midday that the local constabulary heard tell of the attack. Head Constable F.J. Maclaine rushed round to the house and demanded to know why the police had not been notified of the previous night's events.

'Ach,' flustered Heron, 'I didn't want to disturb the police on a Sunday, and besides, your enquiries here might only attract attention.'

The officer insisted on seeing Willie. He climbed the stairs with Heron, entered the darkened bedroom where Willie, more dead than alive, was lying. Maclaine talked to Willie, noting down everything he said. Heron listened in attentively. Quinn, his voice little more than a whisper by now, described his walk home the night before.

'He was a big man, bigger than me .... he was waiting. I think he must have been behind the gate pillar. Then I heard his feet behind me ... and he hit me and went on hitting me...'

'Could you recognise the man, Willie?' the officer asked gently. Quinn seemed not to have heard. His eyes wandered slowly around the room, settled on his step-father, and continued on their way.

'No, I don't know who it was, it was too dark.' Willie slipped into a coma within the hour and died in the early hours of Monday morning.

The blinds were drawn in Flush Hall and , as word of Willie's untimely demise spread around Ards, many local people called in to offer their sympathy to the Herons. The police meanwhile were interviewing every possible witness, following up every lead. Quinn's murder, they concluded, had not been committed on the spur of the moment; the killer had known his movements and lain in wait for him.

But what motive could there have been? Quinn was only a poor clerk in his step-father's factory and though his watch - torn from its chain - was missing, it seemed impossible that the motive for the murder could have been robbery.

Jealousy perhaps? Quinn was about to marry Miss Mary Lavery. Both, though, were well liked in the area and if there had been a disappointed suitor lurking around, then the tightly-knit local community would surely have known about him.

The inquest was held on the Tuesday and a verdict of murder by a person unknown was returned. On Tuesday 18th February 1915, the day Willie Quinn was to be married, his funeral cortege set out from Flush Hall. His final journey was a long one; it had been decided that Willie should be buried in the Quinn family plot in Newry.

A solemn column of men followed the horse-drawn hearse down the street. At its head were Samuel Heron and his son. As the funeral procession made its way slowly through the town, the people of Ards looked on in silence. Near the town's edge a small group of policemen waited. As the hearse dre
w level with them, Head Constable Maclaine steeped forward and bid the driver halt. The mourners and spectators looked on in anticipation. What was happening?

Maclaine approached Samuel Heron Snr. and placed his hand on his shoulder. Heron reddened; the eyes of the crowd were upon him. Maintaining his composure, he told Maclaine, 'I won't hesitate, I will go with you.'

The news spread through a stunned Newtownards. A crowd gathered outside the police station where Heron was being interrogated. Inside, Maclaine was making slow progress with Heron who refused to give a statement and demanded to see a solicitor. He stuck to the story he had told at the inquest: the attack had really been meant for him. Heron claimed to have sacked several workers in recent weeks, one of them must have decided to get even with him. Willie had been the unfortunate victim of a terrible mistake.

After a few hours of fruitless interviewing, Maclaine read the formal charge of murder. Heron replied in a tone of resignation that, 'I was expecting this.' A police 'Black Maria' reversed through the crowd right up to the steps of the station and Heron was bundled into it to be taken to Belfast Prison.

The crowd outside Downpatrick railway station on the 14th July 1915 was enormous; the world and his wife turned out to see the man accused of Willie Quinn's murder. At 1.35 the Belfast train drew into the station and Heron alighted looking spruce and confident. He smiled at several acquaintances in the
e crowd and wished one young lady a 'good morning.' She burst into tears: it was Mary, Willie's fiancee.

Samuel Heron was tried three times. At each trial, the prosecution produced evidence of opportunity and motive. They also had a 'star' witness whose weird story made Heron's guilt seem conclusive.

At each of the trials the defence offered no evidence. Heron was not called upon to account for his movements or defend himself from the allegations made against him. Nor were any other witnesses called on his behalf.

His answer to the charges was that they had not been proved. His counsel, Mr T.W. Brown, contented himself with a reasoned address to the jury and in each case it worked. For all three juries disagreed and, according to tradition, Heron was released.

Juries in Northern Ireland are renowned for their reluctance to convict a man on a capital charge. Ulstermen will not take the responsibility for putting a noose around a man's neck if there is a slightest doubt about his guilt. So it was in the case of Samuel Heron. The doubt was considerable and outweighed the prosecution's carefully constructed case. Under Scottish law the verdict might have been 'not proven.'

Outlining the prosecution's case, the Attorney General, Mr. John Gordon, concentrated on the financial mess in which Heron had landed himself by trying to keep up appearances at Flush Hall. The man in the dock, he said, was under pressure to settle debts totalling £1600 and one of his creditors was none other than Willie Quinn. Willie had inherited some property in Newry from his mother. Heron had been appointed trustee and all rents were paid into his account. As his wedding approached, Willie had asked for an accounting and the prosecution claimed that Heron was in no position to give one, having spent the money.

This was the motive for the murder. Heron, harassed and worried, had snapped under the strain, argued the prosecution. The exposure of the misappropriated rents would have ruined his standing in Ards. Therefore he had every reason for wanting to shut Willie's mouth, even for good.

Motive need not be proven to secure a conviction in a murder case. The judge's duty is to assess the evidence presented, not to speculate on the reasons behind the crime. The Attorney General needed to link Samuel Heron positively with the murder. To do this he brought on his 'star witness' and 'Exhibit A', the murder weapon itself, a heavy wooden kitchen utensil, shaped like a circular mallet and used for mashing potatoes.

The discovery of this beetle and the odd story behind it has stuck to the history of the case. To this day the trial is known as the 'Beetle Murder.'

The first two witnesses called upon were routine. Henry Aicken, a friend of Willie's, related how they had spent part of the evening at the Masonic Hall and then gone on to Wallace's Pub afterwards. Quinn, he said, had set off for home at about 11.30. Two sisters who lived in the cottage attached to Flush Hall, Nellie and Grace Dunn, reported hearing a scream at midnight.

The next witness, however, created a stir in the court. He was Samuel Heron Jnr., called by the prosecution to testify against his own father.

Head in hands and weeping, Heron listened to his son taking the oath. Samuel Jnr's. account of the events made for strange hearing indeed. He had retired for the night at about 10.30, as had his father and step-mother. Not long after this they heard the dogs howling outside. The two Samuels went down below and outside to see what was disturbing them. The father carried his shotgun and, finding no-one in the Hall's grounds, he fired into the air, presumably to scare off any intruders still in the vicinity. Both then returned to bed. At 12.30 the son was wakened by his mother. The father was not in the house. The son descended the staircase once again and met the father coming back into the house, fully dressed. When asked for an explanation, the father said that he had heard the dogs barking again.

This evidence, argued the prosecution, placed Heron within yards of the critically injured Willie Quinn within minutes of the murderous attack. If he had been outside on an innocent errand, how had he not seen or heard his step-son sprawled on the steps and screaming?

Dr. Jamison was called next and seemed ill-at-ease in the witness box. After recounting his version of events on that Sunday, the doctor claimed that he had been unable to leave the house that night to attend to the dying Quinn. 'That was how Dr. Warlock was, unfortunately, brought into the case.' "Why 'unfortunately'?" asked the Attorney General. 'Well,' said Jamison, 'I would have give £20 if I had stayed in my bed that Sunday morning.'

Dr. Warlock gave evidence that Quinn had died from a star-shaped fracture of the skull and a blood clot on the brain.

The sensations in the Heron case came on the second day of the first trial when William McBride was called to give evidence. The defence would later deride McBride as a 'peculiar kind of man.' His story, according to Mr. Brown was 'the most incredible ever told in a witness box.' Incredible, maybe; but that it was startling was beyond doubt. Spectators gasped as McBride gave his testimony and the defence counsel took frantic notes for the cross-examination. McBride was a labourer at the Ulster Print Works; he was also related to Heron, having married his niece. On the Tuesday after the murder , said McBride, Heron took him aside at the factory and confided in him that there was a danger he might be arrested for Willie Quinn's murder. The next day, McBride continued, he received a message to go to Flush Hall immediately. An agitated Heron met him and said, 'If anything happens to me, you may sell the pigeons, also the poultry and take one of the dogs. Take my bicycle and sell it. Give the money to Mrs. Heron.

McBride listened to these odd instructions until Heron seemed to be finished. As he turned to go back to the factory, Heron called him back. 'Wait, I still want you. Look under the tank in the mill chimney as you will find the watch, as, like an old fool, I got it and hid it there.' McBride had assumed that this was Quinn's watch. Again he turned to go back to work, only to be called back. Heron led McBride into the scullery and asked, 'I wonder is there anything they might look for? For instance, this....?' 'This' was the large wooden beetle.

McBride's amazing narrative went on. Heron had tried to wash the beetle under the hot water-tap. McBride had noticed that the thick end of the wooden masher was darkly stained. After a while Heron handed him the beetle with the words, 'You might give it a rub with the brush while I see if anyone is about.'

Upon returning to the scullery his boss and uncle-in-law asked, 'Do you see anything on it?' Because the stain persisted Heron suggested that McBride 'Go down to the Works and get some emery paper.'

Watching his uncle frantically trying to remove the dark stains, McBride suggested that Heron burn the beetle but Heron persisted until the stain eventually came out. Heron was then alleged to have rubbed some chicken-meal over the instrument before placing it in a bucket of mash.

'Remember who I am and who is talking to you,' he warned McBride, 'When you get a chance remove these things. If the police get nothing, they can prove nothing against me.' He then handed

McBride a ten pound note for 'work you have done about the house,' before adding, 'Don't change the note until you get to Belfast.'

All this caused a commotion in court. The noise died down as Mr. Gordon held up 'Exhibit A'. Is this the beetle you have been talking about?' he asked McBride, who peered at it and said, 'Yes.' McBride went on to tell the court that he had become worried about the whole incident and finally decided to tell the police. On the day of the funeral Heron had apparently asked him if he had disposed of the things.' When McBride said no he hadn't, Heron snapped, 'You'll wait until it's too late.'

McBride was then grilled by Mr. Brown. Why had he not produced this evidence at the inquest? The judge, Mr Justice Dodds, sided with the defence and pressed McBride, who replied that he had not wanted to reveal his story until he had obtained legal advice.

The last witness for the prosecution was the eminent pathologist Dr. Robert. M. Bronte from Dublin. He had examined the beetle and a pair of trousers belonging to Heron. On the turn-ups of these trousers he had found blood-stains which looked as though they had been caused by a spurt of blood from an artery. In the head of the beetle he had detected a crack; in it were traces of blood - human blood.

This was the first case in Northern Ireland in which blood analysis was entered as evidence. Before improvements in scientific techniques, it had been difficult to distinguish between human and animal blood. Under cross-examination, Dr. Bronte agreed that the blood could have found it's way into the crack if the beetle had been used for washing bloody clothes.

Mr. Brown told the jury he had no witnesses to call. 'The defence,' he said, 'has no evidence. How could there be? There is no need for Samuel Heron to prove that he did not do this killing.' The defence, he continued, relied on the omissions and failures of the Crown. Firstly he attacked the alleged motive for the crime: that Heron feared Quinn discovering the loss of the rent money. This was nonsense; if it were true, it would not conceal the truth for long because of Quinn's aunts in Newry who also had an interest in the property. They would have discovered any loss.

However, said the defence, there was no loss anyway. Heron had used the money to educate and apprentice Quinn, whom he had supported since his mother's death. As for Heron's debts, they were all well secured and none of the traders in Ards was pressing for payment.

Finally the defence counsel tried to destroy William McBride's evidence by implying that the whole beetle cleaning episode was a fabrication. 'McBride is a peculiar sort of man. He is of inferior station to the accused. Yet he is married to this man's niece.' The defence implied that McBride was envious and resentful of Heron. The eloquent plea ended with Mr.Brown telling the jury that, 'Either McBride is mad or Heron was mad. It is the most incredible story ever told in a witness-box.'

Enough members of the jury were impressed by this line of defence to force the jury to disagree. And so it was at the two subsequent trials. Almost a year after Willie Quinn's death, Samuel Heron was released from Belfast Prison. He returned to Newtownards for a while but found that in such a small community the notoriety he had acquired made life unbearable. Before long he emigrated to Australia where he died.

There are few relics left pertaining to the infamous Newtownards 'Beetle Murder.' The beetle itself was lost after the trials. Even the scene of the crime, Flush Hall, has disappeared, demolished to clear space for the new Scrabo Estate.

> *In the peaceful town of Newtownards,*
> *A few miles from Belfast*
> *An awful crime has taken place*
> *Which makes people stand aghast.*
>
> *That such a deed on Sunday morn*
> *Could be planned and carried out*
> *Has filled with horror and dismay*
> *All the country round about*
>
> *The unhappy victim, Willie Quinn,*
> *whose age was twenty-three,*
> *Was as quiet and inoffensive a youth,*
> *As one could wish to see.*
>
> *His late residence it is called Flush Hall,*
> *Along the Scrabo Road,*
> *Where peace and comfort seemed to dwell*
> *In that well-to-do abode.*

He had such a host of pals and chums
That no-one ever dreamt
He had a single enemy
That would this vile deed attempt.

But going home at Sunday's dawn,
Some villain lay in wait
And murderously assaulted him,
As he entered by the gate.

Then left the lad in agony,
On his hands and knees to crawl
And to reach four hours afterwards
The bell-pull at the Hall.

His mournful death occurred next day
And cast quite a pall of gloom
That such a bright and social lad
Should meet with such a doom.

There are memories quite pathetic
Of the youth now passed away;
He was buried on the morn that
Should have been his wedding day.

The wicked wretch who did this deed,
Must hang his head in shame;
Where ere he be upon this earth
He bears the brand of Cain.

Dread and fear will fill his memory
And make a hell within,
And he will rue the Sunday morn
He murdered Willie Quinn.

The Trial of The Fourth Lord Santry
27th April 1739

Although the fourth Lord Santry was not hanged, I have decided to include his case in this book because of the rare insight it gives us into our penal past. It also quite interesting per se. I came across the story of Santry while researching the Lords Chancellor of Ireland. What attracted me to it was the detail and the order in which the trial was conducted. It all happened during the reign of George II. In the spring of 1739 Henry the fourth Lord Santry was put on trial for the murder of Laughlin Murphy at Palmerstown near Dublin. Santry, 'wild young nobleman' that he was, was a member of the 'Hell Fire Club', an organisation dedicated to heavy drinking, obscenity, profligacy and orgies. After one drinking session Santry quarrelled with Murphy, drew his sword and ran him through. Murphy died almost seven weeks later. Only then was Santry arrested for murder. The trial began at 6 am on 27th April 1739. Santry was asked how he would be tried and replied, 'By God and my peers.' The defence argued that Murphy's death had been caused by disease but Santry was found guilty of murder. Strings were pulled on Santry's behalf and he was reprieved and ultimately pardoned. If the boot had been on the other foot, Murphy could have expected no such mercy. But let us return to the trial. Security was heavy in Dublin that morning. A regiment of soldiers was sent to College Green and a company of battleaxe guards lined the avenues leading to Parliament House. The police were also out in force. At 7.30 am the 29-year-old Santry arrived by hackney coach at the house of Commons in the company of the High Sheriff of the City of Dublin. The lower house, being larger, had been preferred to the upper house for the state trial. The time set for the trial to begin seems unnecessarily greatly. It must have been intended to avoid publicity or any popular demonstrations for or against the prisoner. In any case, Lord Wyndham, the Lord Chancellor, did not turn up at Parliament House on St Stephen's Green until 10 am. The pageantry merits a detailed description. The judges, wearing scarlet robes, and the King-of-Arms went to the Lord Chancellor's residence on St Stephen' Green to wait on him as Lord High Steward and escort him to the High Court of Parliament. The King-of-Arms and the Usher of the Black Rod were also robed. The Sergeant-at-Arms had the Mace. The procession from the Lord

Chancellor's residence to the coaches drawn up before it was a magnificent spectacle. Twelve gentlemen marched bareheaded, two by two; then came the Sergeant-at-Arms and the Seal Bearer, also uncovered, one carrying the Mace and the other the Purse. His Grace the Lord High Steward, in his robes and attended by the train bearers, was supported on his right by the Ulster King-of-Arms and on his left by the Usher of the Black Rod; then came the Chief Justices and other judges. The coaches moved off. The coach bearing the Lord High Steward was drawn by six horses, the others by three. When the procession reached College Green it was met by four more miscarrying sergeants. The company then entered the Court, in which the peers were already seated, in order of seniority. A Chair-of-State, beneath a rich canopy and a step higher than the other peers' seats, had been prepared for Wyndam. After passing said peers, bowing left and right as he went, he took his place to his right. The Clerk of the Crown of the King's Commission to the Chancellor, made their references to his Grace, approaching him and kneeling. The Clerk of the Crown in Chancery then presented the commission to his Grace, who, in turn, handed it to the Clerk of the Crown of the King's Bench. They bowed thrice and returned to the table. The Sergeant-at-Arms called 'ooze' thrice and the Clerk of the Crown of the King's Bench read aloud the Commission. As he did this, the Lords stood uncovered. Once this was done, His Grace bowed to the peers, who returned the salute and sat down again. The King-of-Arms and the Usher of the Black Rod then gave ... and, on their knees, jointly presented the White Staff to his Grace. The Lord High Steward then returned the staff to the Usher of the Black Rod who held it during the trial. Then the King-of-Arms stood to the right and the Usher of the Black Rod, holding the staff, to the left of his Grace

The peers then took their places on the benches on either side, according to seniority. When the charge had been read, the Clerk of the Crown asked His Lordship to plead 'not guilty'. He was then asked how he would be tried and replied, 'By God and my peers.' The Rt Rev Dr. Rendle, Bishop of Derry, remarked, 'I never beheld a sight so awful and majestic and dreadfully beautiful in my life; nothing was ever performed with so much solemnity, silence, and dignity before in any country.' How time changes attitudes! Lord William Neville, one of the 'Jabez Balfour Gang', who was sent to Parkhurst Prison in 1889 for commercial fraud, laments in 'Penal servitude', written after his release in 1901, that when he was arrested 'there was no rallying around of my fellow Lords for encouragement, but on the contrary, most of my old friends would have nothing to do with me.' When he was eventually released a few true friends did stand by him, though. But how attitudes changed in the 162 years between the two cases! Lord Chancellor Jocelyn conducted the trial in 1743 of Nicholas the Fifth Viscount Netterville for the murder of Michael Walsh in County Meath. Anyone who had attended both trials, ie those of Santry and Netterville, might have experienced a certain feeling of deja vu for very much the same produce was followed with very much the same outcome. Owing to the deaths of the two main witnesses, whose depositions were rejected as evidence, the prosecution failed. The Lord Steward concluded that, 'the house having heard all the evidence, the question was whether Nicholas Lord Netterville is guilty of the felony treason and murder where of he stands indicated or not guilty.' The peers were then called, beginning with the youngest baron who, when stood in his place and uncovered, laid his right hand on his breast and declared, 'Lord Netterville not guilty, upon my honour.' The Lord Steward then broke the White Staff and adjourned the House.

Thomas Russell
The Man From God Knows Where

One of the most notable men to be hanged after the United Irishmen's rebellion of 1798 was Thomas Russell. Russell was born in
County Cork in 1767. He joined the British Army but left it after five
years and returned to Ireland. He met Wolfe Tone, whose determi-
nation to 'break the connection with England' he shared, and the
two became closest friends and founder members of the United
Irishmen. Russell became the organisations chief organiser and
commander in County Down. After his capture he was taken to
Kilmainham Jail in Dublin and from there to Downpatrick Jail where
he was hanged on 19th October 1803.

Florence M. Wilson wrote the following poem entitled;

THE MAN FROM GOD KNOWS WHERE

Into our townland' on a night of snow
Came a man from God knows where.
None of us bade him stay nor go,
Nor deemed him friend, nor damned him foe,
But we stabled his big roan mare;
For in our townland' were decent folk,
An' if he didn't speak, why none of us spoke.
An' we sat till the fire burned low.

We're a civil sort in our wee place,
So we made the circle wide
Round Andy Lemon's cheerful blaze,
An' wished the man his len'th o' days,
An' a good end to his ride.
He smiled in under his slouchy hat.
Says he, 'there's a bit of a joke in that,
For we ride different ways.'

The whiles we smoked we watched him stare
From his seat ... the glow.
I nudged Joe Moore, 'You wouldn't dare

To ask him who he's meeting there,
Or how far he has to go.'
But Joe wouldn't dare, nor Wully Scott.
An' he took no drink, neither hot nor cold,
This man from God knows where.

It was closin' time, an' late forbye,
When us ones braved the air.
I never saw worse (may I live or die)
Than the sleet that night, an' I says, says I,
'You'll find he's for stoppin' there.'
But at screek o' day, through the gable pane,
I watched him spur in the peltin' rain,
An' I juked his rovin' eye.

Two winters more, then the trouble year
When the best that man could feel
Was the pike he kept in hidlin's near,
Till the blood o' hate an' the blood o' fear
Would be redder nor rust on the steel.
Us ones quit from mindin' the farms,
Let them take what we give wi' the weight o' our arms
From Saintfield to Kilkeel.

In the timeo' the hurry we had to lead
We all of us fought with the rest,
An' if e'er a one shook like a tremblin' reed,
None of us give neither hint nor heed,
Nor ever even we'd guessed.
We men of the North had a word to say,
An' we said it then, in our own dour way,
An' we spoke as we thought was best.

All Ulster over, the weemen cried
For the stan'in' crops on the lan'.
Many's the sweetheart, many's the bride
Would liefer ha' mourned her lone by her man.
But us ones weathered the thick of of it,
An' we used to dander along along, an' sit
In Andy's side by side.

130

What with discoorse goin' to and fro,
The night would be wearin' thin,
Yet never so late when we rose to go
But someone would say, 'Do ye min' thon snow,
Anis the man that came wanderin' in?'
And we be to fall to the talk again,
If by any chance he was one o' them,
The man who went like the win'.

Well, 'twas gettin' on past the heat o' the year
When I rode to Newtown fair;
I sold as I could (the dealers were near -
Only three pounds eight for the innish steer,
An' nothin' at all for the mare).
I met McKee in the throng o' the street;
Says he, 'The grass has grown under our feet
Since they hanged young Warwick here.'

And he told me that Boney had promised help
To a man in Dublin town.
Says he, 'If ye've laid the pike on the shelf,
Ye'd better go home hot-fut by yourself,
An' polish the old girl down.'
So by Comber Road I trotted the grey
And never cut corn till Killyleagh
Stood plain on the risin' ground.

For a wheen o' days we sat waitin' the word
To rise an' go at it like men.
But no French ships sailed into Claughey Bay
And we heard the black news on a harvest day
That the cause was lost again;
And Joey and me, and Wully Boy Scott,
We agreed to ourselves we'd as lief as not
Ha' been found in the thick o' the slain.

By Downpartick jail I was bound to fare
On a day I'll remember, feth;
For when I came to the prison square
The people were waitin' in hundreds there,

An' you would't hear stir not breath,
For the sodgers were standing, grim and tall,
An 'a man stepped out for death.

I was brave and near to the edge of the throng,
Yet I knowed the face again,
An' I knowed the set, an I knowed the walk,
An' the sound of the strange up-country talk,
For he spoke out right an 'plain.
Then he bowed his head to the swingin rope,
An 'Amen' to his dyin' prayer
That the wrong would cease an' the right prevail,
For that man that they hanged at Downpatrick Jail
Was the man from God-knows where!

In Conclusion

We have looked at the differences throughout the years about Capital Punishment, and its these attitudes and the so called modern view to the same type of offence today. In the thirty seven years of Henry VIII's reign we saw that roughly 72,000 individuals were hung, it was in the beginning of the nineteenth century that there was 222 capital offences e.g., stealing a pocket handkerchief, shooting a rabbit etc. When we looked at the convict at Wicklow in 1738 and when we consider his speech, one cannot disagree with him, he has a valid point. And when we looked at the contents of the letters to the Lord Mayor of London in 1786, which states, at Tyburn alone they were hanging people in twenty's at a time. Last but not least I have tackled the whole issue of Capital Punishment from a Christian point of view. There were literally hundreds of people executed during the reign of Henry VIII, not only in London, but Wales, Scotland, and Ireland in particular. History tells us that a high percentage was executed because he or she was a Catholic, and in the reign of "Bloody Mary" people were hung for being Protestant.

Although we no longer have the Death Penalty in the British Isles or Ireland in 1994, for some twenty five years many different innocent individuals are being executed by the paramilitaries just because he or she is a Catholic or Protestant.

I will end with the following:-In the Belfast Telegraph, October 4th 1993, the headlines read,"Shankill Butcher, Robert Bates, who was jailed for natural life, had been freed from prison on parole. He was convicted in 1979 for 10 murders. Sentencing Bates and fellow ringleader William Moore, who was guilty of 11 Murders, the Judge said, "I see no reason, what ever, apart from terminal illness, why either of you should ever released. The fact speak for themselves and will remain forever a monument to blind sectarian bigotry".

The killers, eleven in all, used knives, blades and hatchets to earn themselves the macabre title of the Shankill Butchers and carried out some of the most horrific murders of 'the Troubles.' They cruised the streets to find their victims, torturing them before slashing their necks and faces with butcher knives. Their blows were so savage that in several cases they almost decapitated their victims, many of whom were Catholics.

The points I would like to make are these, during King Henry VIII reign you would have been hung for stealing a silk handkerchief or shooting a rabbit, here we have individuals who are guilty of eleven murders, and there is talk of their releases. By not hanging this type of criminal we do offer them a chance to accept God's grace, and Christ as their saviour. Only He can forgive them and lighten their conscience.

In the Book of Acts, Chapter 7, verses 58 - 59, we read of young men laying down their coats at a young man's feet called Saul (later to be called Paul), as they stoned Stephen to death, and in Acts, Chapter 9, verse 1., he had got letters from the high priest so that he could imprison Christians. Most would have been tortured and put to death, some were thrown to wild beasts. The Lord Jesus Christ who forgave a murderer like Paul, has grace to forgive the Shankill Road Butchers and people like them.

But then there is the negative aspect to the problem. What more can the authorities do to this type of criminal if they decide to kill another inmate or prison officer? What if they are conning the whole system? We would be filling our towns and city's with potential time bombs. Do I have an answer? 'No.' Do you?